"Most books on mental health avail[able are] theoretical or written by individuals who are antagonistic toward the organized church. A Brave Life is written autobiographically by a woman who grew up in the church and still loves the church though she has experienced its failures and insensitivity. I appreciate the grace with which she relates how the church failed her, the clarity with which she shares her struggle with guilt and shame, and the candidness with which she tells her journey to mental health. Every person in ministry, courageous enough to read A Brave Life, will recognize the need to become more caring toward adults within their ministry who evidence indications of childhood trauma."

–AL MAGNUSON
retired executive minister, Converge Heartland

"Having read her previous two books, I was familiar with Janyne's writing style, the basic direction taken, and her written voice. I enjoyed the first two books and gleaned direction and healing by reading them. But, the power that A Brave Life had on my psychological wellbeing cannot be overstated. I vividly recall the point in the book where Janyne captured my wounded heart. Her shared experience and crafty storytelling captured my literary mind and wielded an emotional sword that pricked my heart, allowing me to come face to face with my need to pursue opportunities to walk the path to healing. I shall be eternally grateful.

"As an educator and church minister for over thirty years, I have read and reviewed countless books on spiritual matters. The difference between A Brave Life and other books is Janyne's ability to weave her personal story into a familiar character, Dorothy, and make relevant connections to everyone's life. I believe, no matter where you are in your healing journey, this book will serve as a catalyst for wholeness."

–MALCOLM L. MCGUIRE, Ed. D.
Educator and Curriculum Specialist

"Throughout Janyne's story there were many struggles that I and other Christians I know have experienced that prevented us from experiencing the full scope of joy and peace God offers. A Brave Life gives hope. By sharing her story Janyne has opened up the conversation. Let's tear down the lies that hold our minds and hearts captive. Let's live in the Light!"

–ROSIE LOLESS
Educator

"Author Janyne McConnaughey writes out of her own life experiences and succeeds in explaining the complex feelings and fantasies that surround suicidal thoughts. In a direct, nonjudgmental and loving voice, she offers affirmations and suggestions for those harboring life-ending thoughts. Families and friends of those suffering will glean wisdom, as well, and after reading this important book, will be better able to assist those loved ones who are at risk. McConnaughey is to be commended for coming out of the darkness to shine a light on issues that usually remain hidden; issues that wreak chaos and damage to individuals who carry childhood pain long into adulthood. How I wish everyone could have access to this profound book as its message of healing and recovery are urgently needed in our world."

–SUSAN JENKINS
educator and author (*Scandalon*)

"Trauma is about fear and hurting. Healing is about relationship and safety. Relationship needs hope and faith. In this book, Janyne, Non-Janyne, Jane, and all the children we have come to love from her first two books, come together to teach us about resilience. All of the beautiful, vulnerable voices tell a difficult truth that leaves the reader feeling more connected to his/her faith."

–MELISSA SADIN, EdD, MAT, M.Ed.

"In her third book, Janyne addresses what her readers have been thinking, 'How did Dissociative Identity Disorder affect her day-to-day life as an adult?' In her captivating story-telling way, Janyne answers that question as she takes us along on the journey of her sometimes-confused life that ultimately leads to her Emerald City."

–LESLIE R. MIKESELL, Ph.D.

"This engaging and poignant book is an invaluable window into childhood trauma, dissociative disorder, and the heart of Jesus. It has fine-tuned my radar and helped me to recognize and relate more effectively to congregants whether we're doing the work of the church or they are seeking counseling. The failure of the church to protect and support Janyne at critical times in her life is truly heartbreaking. We can do better; we must do better! This book can school us to be more aware, more sensitive, more like Jesus to children and adults who have suffered trauma. In this page turner, Janyne cleverly weaves her story with Dorothy of Oz in a way that is both illuminating and entertaining. I highly recommend it for anyone in ministry."

–REV. SUSAN ARMSTRONG
D.M.A., Pastor of Care and Discipleship, Reynoldsburg, OH
Church of the Nazarene

A BRAVE LIFE

SURVIVAL, RESILIENCE, FAITH *and* HOPE
after CHILDHOOD TRAUMA

Janyne McConnaughey, Ph.D.

CLADACH
Publishing

Lots of people want to ride with you in the limo,
but what you want is someone who will take the
bus with you when the limo breaks down.

–Oprah Winfrey

Dedicated to my friend

Paula Scarbrough

who was willing to "ride the bus" with
me as my "limo" of carefully constructed
coping mechanisms began to break down.
Her unconditional acceptance opened the
door for me to access healing. She is
representative of all my friends, both old
and new, who have supported me before and
after the writing of *BRAVE*, to which
this book is a prequel.
My friends help me to be brave!

A Brave Life

CONTENTS

FOREWORD

Owning our story can be hard but not nearly as difficult as spending our lives running from it. Embracing our vulnerabilities is risky but not nearly as dangerous as giving up on love and belonging and joy—the experiences that make us the most vulnerable. Only when we are brave enough to explore the darkness will we discover the infinite power of our light.

—Brené Brown

We're generally a society that glamorizes comfort, carefully measures behavior, and divorces ourselves of any person or process that threatens (in reality or perception) to unravel the neatly formed lives we diligently craft for ourselves. In some ways there's a hurting child self in each of us, a little voice pointing to the places where we are vulnerable, wanting desperately to be seen and accepted, but also holding back.

Even when we have the most ideal parents, some emotional and relational trauma enters into our lives. What we do with that, how we learn to cope, becomes a part of who we are. It's a rare gift to find acceptance in secure relationships, learning to nurture joy through appreciation and gratitude that leads us to a healthy sense of resilience.

Hurt happens in community; so too does the messy, scary work of healing. When the nature of true love gets twisted up into complex trauma, the response requires a great deal of courage. This courage risks the discomfort of leaning into relationship, looking beyond behavior with a curiosity that asks, "What happened here?"—knowing that when messy is authentic, it's a beautiful part of the process.

In this book, Janyne pushes back the curtain to reveal the real courage it takes to say, "I'm not OK." May her courage inspire us to find safe spaces for ourselves and be those safe spaces for others.

Kiersten Adkins, M.A., LPC
Executive Director, Pathway to Hope

INTRODUCTION
THE EMERALD CITY
OF ABUNDANT LIFE

The most curious things about [the Silver Shoes] is that they can carry you to any place in the world in three steps, and each step will be made in the wink of an eye.

—Oz[1]

Characters from my favorite childhood books often participate in the writing process; and on this day, Alice of Wonderland and Dorothy of Oz were in a heated discussion with Non Janyne,[2] one of my adult selves. They had come to an impasse as to how to introduce this three-part book.

Dorothy was chosen to participate in this book because she is much like my child self, Jeannie, who spent a significant amount of time searching for answers. Dorothy thought if she reached the Emerald City and met the Wizard of Oz, he would solve all her problems. My lifelong search for answers felt much

---

1. Quotes attributed to Oz are from the book, *The Wonderful Wizard of Oz* by Frank L. Baum, originally published in 1900. There are many differences between the book and the 1939 movie based on the book. For instance, in the movie the silver shoes were changed to ruby slippers and the Tin Woodman (described as the tin man in the book) is named the Tin Man (the name used here unless quoting the book). For a short book summary and comparison see: Rosales, R., "The Wonderful Wizard of Oz: What the Movie Got Wrong," Bookriot Blog (May, 31, 2017). Retrieved from https://bookriot.com/2017/05/31/the-wonderful-wizard-of-oz-what-the-movie-got-wrong/

2. In this book, unless otherwise indicated, the names Janyne, Jane, and Non Janyne refer to the three dissociative adult selves identified as the Three Chairs in *BRAVE*.

like Dorothy's quest; and while writing this book, her input was deeply appreciated.

During the writing of this Introduction, Alice (who would not be part of this book) dropped by to check on progress. Eager to step through the looking glass into the *next* book, and wanting to keep things moving, she shot a sideways glance at Non Janyne (the adult self almost always in charge), and said, "You know, this is Dorothy's book. She can plan it any way she wants."

"Yes, I can...." Dorothy said with both hesitation and determination, while looking sideways at Non Janyne.

Sensing the impasse, the other two adult selves, Janyne and Jane entered the room with a simultaneous laugh and sigh. They had come to provide the necessary balance.

Jane, always concerned about the feelings of others, said, "Non Janyne means no harm; she just wants to make sure the readers understand the purpose for the book. This is a story about surviving and how we subconsciously hid all our traumatic memories.[3] Telling this story will take all of us, because it was the result of childhood experiences. Except in the ways that trauma lived on in our life, our struggles were not adult problems."

---

3. American Psychiatric Association. *Diagnostic and Statistical Manual of Mental Disorders: DSM-5* (Arlington, VA: American Psychiatric Association, 2013)
Note: "Trauma," as defined in the DSM-5 requires "actual or threatened death, serious injury, or sexual violence." In this book, the use of the word "trauma" (acknowledging trauma as inherently subjective) broadens this definition to include any situation which causes an individual to feel threatened physically or emotionally, feel powerless, and/or overwhelms the capacity to cope (resulting in lasting adverse effects on wellbeing and ability to function). This expansion is essential when considering how an adult's adverse experiences during childhood increase the likelihood of registering events later in life as traumatic.

"You're so right," Janyne said. "There were many good experiences in our adult life. No one could have known how you struggled. People only saw my adventures and Non Janyne's accomplishments, but there was so much more happening behind all that and beneath the surface. Yes, tell the story!"

"Yes!" Dorothy agreed, looking at the three adults. "The book needs all of you or it won't feel balanced. And *my* role will be to keep us on the Yellow Brick Road to the Emerald City."

At the mention of the Emerald City, Janyne (usually bursting with ideas) sent the conversation in a new direction with her inspirations about the book cover.

"Oh! The Emerald City is like Seattle, which is where we want to go eventually. They call Seattle the Emerald City, you know. The Yellow Brick Road is a path, and our path to healing was writing. I have a picture of a bright yellow typewriter we can use to symbolize our writing."

And with that, she ran off to search for the picture of the typewriter.

Dorothy, not yet accustomed to these spontaneous epiphanies so typical of Janyne, turned now to Non Janyne with a suggestion: "Since this is the adult book, why don't *you* begin—by relaying the essential information? The children can go play while the adults write." (In hindsight, this was Dorothy's near-fatal error. Non Janyne stepped in and the voices of the children vanished. Eventually this decision would be the cause of our having to rewrite the book.)

SEVERAL MONTHS LATER

Sometimes Non Janyne's voice required editing after sending a manuscript. After reading the first manuscript of this book, my publisher sent a complimentary message about the writing, but also said: "It feels like you lost your writer's voice."

I had. It was true…. But why?

The answer surprised me. Even after I had sat on a therapy couch for three years and figured out that my mental health issues were not adult problems, I sent the children away while Non Janyne started writing. And she analyzed the book to death. She *did* acknowledge the childhood roots of the problem, and even included a few essential stories, but the voices of the children were missing—especially the voice of one particular child self.

While reading my publisher's words, it felt as if Non Janyne raised her hand and confessed. Her analysis, though essential for healing, had overwhelmed the book. We had a problem.

The problem wasn't what we understood; it was what we didn't yet know. A subconsciously buried memory kept Non Janyne preoccupied with analyzing—because she knew something didn't make sense. She tried to figure out the "un-figure-out-able." The attempt to reconcile my spiritual journey with childhood experiences in the church needed the voice of a child self who still held tightly to the memory of a conversation that changed everything.

Meanwhile, upon receiving an invitation to speak at a Christian university psychology department event, the memory began to rumble. This afforded the opportunity to do some necessary processing. (God is like that. My month-long, arduous preparation for the presentation had little to do with the slide show and everything to do with the memory attempting to dislodge itself.) This memory, which Ten tells in the Prologue, changed this book into what you are now reading.

HOW THE BOOK CHANGED

"I finally get it!" Non Janyne announced. "The intent of this book was to help the church better understand those who have experienced childhood trauma (See Addendum 6: Trauma-Informed Church Ministries). Even after rewriting, it still meets the original objectives and parts of the Introduction still work. After all, I did work very hard on it." (Though she accepted the need to rewrite, Non Janyne did feel slightly rebuffed.)

Yes, you did, Non Janyne. And all your work is not lost!

~

The story told in this prequel takes place after childhood but before the story told in *BRAVE: A Personal Story of Healing Childhood Trauma* (see Addendum I: A Synopsis of *BRAVE*). Through these stories of my adult life, you, the reader, will be able to:

1. Grasp how surviving (and even succeeding) despite the effects of adverse childhood experiences[4], can be mistaken as thriving by others but sensed as emptiness and spiritual failure or worthlessness by survivors.

2. Gain insights into the way insecure attachment, childhood trauma, and incorrect internalized messages subconsciously affect every facet of life (emotional, relational, spiritual, academic, professional, and physical), often causing survivors' actions to be misjudged.

3. Recognize the importance of supportive nonjudgmental relationships (leaders / family / friends) that encourage survivors to seek professional help for healing childhood trauma.

It is a mistake to deny or distance ourselves from our own painful emotions. The traumatized emotions of my child self often seemed like overwhelming spiritual turmoil. This was not the case. The inexplicable emotions, depression, dependence on others,

---

4. See Addendum 3, ACEs Research, for information on the effects Adverse Childhood Experiences (ACE).

anxiety, panic attacks, professional struggles, sense of watching life from a distance, and "spiritual failures" all had causes. These causes were subconsciously buried, and I built a life narrative out of the bits and pieces I allowed myself to remember.

All my life I avoided seeking professional help for healing, partly because of a heroic determination to live above and hide the pain, but also because of a lack of knowledge about the effects of trauma. Another big deterrent was the stigma surrounding mental health (in society and in the church).

The spiritual path for survivors of childhood abuse is often fraught with discouragement and pain. While the church proclaimed faith in God as sufficient for all my needs, faith didn't solve the inner turmoil. The effects of abuse did feel like spiritual failure. And the very scriptures which should have given hope, felt like condemnation.

Believing the church held the answer to the pain now seems illogical since those proclaiming to be "faithful followers of Jesus" caused most of the abuse. Despite this, many people of the church were a crucial part of my survival as both a child and an adult—something I try to demonstrate in this book while still saying, "We can do better."

I have written this book out of a desire for the church to better understand the effects of childhood trauma, and to help the hurting seek the necessary help to free themselves from their unhealed stories. Only healing will bring abundant life. Living

---

5. The words/terms "abundance" and "abundant living" refer to a life full of joy and strength for soul, mind, and body. This includes, but is not limited to, the spiritual. Abundant living contrasts with feelings of unworthiness, emptiness, and dissatisfaction which rob an individual of the ability to embrace emotions, be fully present in life and relationships, and recognize and make necessary changes while seeking meaning and purpose.

above emotional pain is not the same as abundant life."[5]

~

As Non Janyne read her introduction, all the parts of my dissociative system gathered around her. Since experiencing healing (described in *BRAVE*), my daily life has become a "whole person" event. But even now, writing is still a "group effort." Every part of my inner self has a distinctive voice which must be included if my writer's voice is to be heard fully.

When people ask me "Do you feel integrated now?" I understand. There are two schools of thought concerning the healing of dissociative disorders. One strives for the personality to become completely united in one, while the other appears more like cooperation. For me, it is both/and. In trying to find the golden ticket of full integration, much of who I am and have been, seems to lose value. Yet, walking around in pieces is confusing to everyone around me.

Writing is different from daily life and interactions. It allows, and requires, every part of me to have a voice. Without the interweaving my readers appreciate, my story would be flat and lifeless. So, in this book as in the previous two, the many voices will remain—all of me, every part of me. We do try to not confuse our readers who have only ever experienced "oneness." We understand that hearing from several "voices" can sometimes cause bewilderment.

The truth is, though, for all of us "oneness" is somewhat of an illusion. All people play various roles, they just don't develop full personalities for those roles. But that discussion is for the next book. At minimum, everyone has a child self, but we are often far more complicated than we imagine.

As we travel down the Yellow Brick Road, the present story will be told with the perspective of healed hindsight and in the voices of my three adult selves (Non Janyne, Janyne, and Jane), occasional cameo appearances by my various child selves, as well as the "guest appearance" of Dorothy of Oz. The personalities of the adults develop along the way, and their interactions display a healed cooperation not present at the beginning of *BRAVE*. I am letting my readers get to know these three parts of me who lived my adult life along with those who preceded them.

All the parts of Janyne before "splitting":
Infant
Two
Three
Four
Five
And the added parts after "splitting":
Six (both The One Who Lives and The One
Who Cries)
Seven (Girl with the Hammer and Keeper of the
Cave of Memories)
Eight (Problem Solver and Girl in the Basement
of Shame—now moved to the Attic of Hope)
Nine (Warrior and Storyteller)
Ten (Older Sibling and Comforter)
Teens Janyne and Jane
Young Adults Janyne and Jane
The Three Chairs (Non Janyne, Jane, and Janyne)

Come join us on the Porch. Everyone is waiting....

PROLOGUE
GATHERING ON THE PORCH

Each of the child, teen, young adult, and adult selves claimed a spot in the large, screened-in porch built by the seven-year-old Girl with the Hammer. Soon everyone had settled into seats in the comfy chairs or porch swings. The evening air cooled as the sun slipped into the night. The Comforter pulled blankets out of a large trunk—soft, cozy blankets.

"There is a problem with the book," Non Janyne began.

"We know!" everyone exclaimed in unison.

Someone laughed and Non Janyne sighed. "Yes, I know. It was my fault. I analyzed too much."

Non Janyne's younger self, the eight-year-old Problem Solver agreed but said, "You were processing. We can fix it. The Storyteller will help us."

The nine-year-old Storyteller smiled, then she looked thoughtfully at Ten. "We just didn't know your story yet, Ten. And Non Janyne got all lost trying to figure out what she didn't know."

Everyone turned to Ten (the Older Sibling). Sensing the need for an explanation, she began. "All the other stories were about the awful things that happened to us. But all I did was make a mistake by breaking a promise."

Now everyone looked confused. The Comforter appeared sad and for once seemed to be at a loss for how to help. Finally she shrugged and said, "Maybe you just need to tell the story."

"OK," her twin agreed. "I was ten ... well, obviously."

Someone laughed again—not a mean laugh, more like an adoring laugh. Non Janyne scanned the room to identify the source, to no avail.

Ten continued. "Well, I wasn't always ten in age, but I'm still named Ten. It's complicated. We moved, and it felt lonely without friends. *Something* had happened that I promised not to tell about. During summer camp, though, everyone was singing around the campfire and it felt wonderful. It felt like God was right there, and it would be OK to talk to someone. So, I tried to talk to a camp counselor. But when she heard my story, she *flinched*."

Everyone shuddered.

(Every part of me feared seeing someone flinch. Later, during therapy, each of my child selves at some point thanked Dr. Sue[6] for not flinching.)

"Yeah, the camp counselor flinched. I made an awful mistake. Telling is always a mistake. She said it was a lie. She said I should never say horrible things like that about someone."

Abruptly, Five jumped up and demanded, "Why did the counselor say that?"

Adult Jane, who was sitting next to Five, pulled her onto her lap. Five peered up at her and said, "Adults lie, they make children lie, and then when we tell the truth, we get in trouble. That makes me mad."

Everyone murmured in agreement. They knew the story Five told about the lie the bad father told after the birthday party (described in my previous book, *Jeannie's BRAVE Childhood*).

Ten looked at Five with sadness in her eyes. "The bad father said you were lying. This time, the camp counselor told me to

---

6. "Dr. Sue" refers to my therapist, Susan M. Kwiecien, Ph.D., LMFT, EMDR II, Retired. The foreword she wrote for *BRAVE* is available in Addendum 2.

confess that I was lying and ask Jesus to forgive me. She said Jesus could then come and live in my heart and save me."

Five wiggled out of Jane's lap and stood in front of Ten. "What did you do?" she asked.

Ten began crying. "I told her I lied. And in telling her that, I was lying against myself. Five, you were stronger than I was. You refused to tell a lie against yourself."

The ten-year-old twins were swinging together in the porch swing so wildly it almost knocked Five over. The Comforter whispered an apology as the Older Sibling lifted Five onto the swing between them.

Five said, "You didn't have a choice. It would have gone very badly for you. But what happened next?"

Looking relieved that Five understood, Ten answered, "She said to repeat after her and ask forgiveness for sinning and then ask Jesus to come into my heart."

"Did you do that?" Five asked.

"Yes. It didn't matter by that point; she didn't believe me anyway. But I didn't feel any better—maybe worse."

JESUS HELPS TEN UNDERSTAND SIN[7]

Everyone watched with surprise as a dark-haired man walked across the porch and kneeled in front of the swing which had now stopped its frenzied rocking. He gazed deeply into Ten's eyes and said, "I loved you from the moment you were created, and I

---

7. Though my readers are from various theological backgrounds, this discussion of sin is informed by my Wesleyan heritage and can be summed up in these words: "We can say that sin is, at its essence, anti-love, and that love, at its essence, leaves no room for sin." See Leclerc, D., *How Do We Define Sin? Essential Beliefs: A Wesleyan Primer*. Eds. Maddix, M. & Leclerc, D. (Beacon Hill Press, Kansas City, Kansas, 2016).

am always with you. You didn't have to ask me to be with you—I have always been there."

At these words, Ten's deep emotional distress began spilling out in the space between them.

"But I lied. I didn't lie, but then did lie, by telling a lie against myself. I didn't sin, but then did sin, to save myself from the counselor not believing me. I broke a promise. I had promised not to tell. Was it a sin to break the promise? I needed someone to care; but it *was* a promise. Maybe that is the sin. Or is sin the bad things I let happen to me? Maybe it was all sin."

The Comforter and Five moved, and Jesus sat next to Ten. He held her in the gently rocking porch swing. The whole porch remained silent. In fact, it seemed the world fell silent.

"Ten, do you know the Ten Commandments?"

"Everyone knows them," Ten answered and then wondered if the answer was a bit abrupt. She added, "That is why I know I shouldn't lie."

"Yes, but do you know why they were given to the Israelites?"

Ten thought the answer was obvious. "So they wouldn't do bad things."

Jesus smiled. "That is what they became—rules. The intent was for them to be a guide that would help people in their relationships with God and each other. They were ways to demonstrate love to God and other people—cautions about those things that harm relationships."

Ten looked thoughtful. "Then that's why you said the greatest commandment was to love God and our neighbor?"

"That's right, Ten. Now, I will ask another question, a difficult but important question: What was the very worst part about all the terrible things that happened to you?"

Ten thought hard for a moment. Then with a sob she said, "I didn't know who to trust. Not even you or Dr. Sue. Trusting was so difficult. I got it wrong a lot."

Jesus held Ten tightly. "Yes, without trust, life is full of problems. You were created for relationship—with God and with others. Children who are fully loved, protected, and cared for build trust and can love and accept love because they feel safe.... You never felt safe, though, did you?"

"No. I didn't feel safe. And I lied to protect myself. I did my best to follow the other commandments, but lying was important to me. Non Janyne could stop us from lying, though."

"You did try, Ten. At camp you lied because of a false accusation by an adult who should have stepped in to love and protect you. This is all about relationships. Without adequate protection, children learn they have to take care of themselves. With few options, lying was your best choice."

"I did lie a lot. But you mean, you understand?" Ten looked surprised. "I thought you hated sin."

"I hate the ways that non-loving choices damage people and their relationships with others and with God. Ten, you did nothing wrong. You were caring for yourself—something you learned to do as a small child. When this is just about the commandment, the reason for the commandment is lost—love one another. When you got older and learned other strategies, you set lying aside. You understood how it damaged relationships and trust."

With grace beyond her years Ten said, "I don't think the camp counselor meant to hurt me."

Jesus smiled fondly at Ten. "No, she didn't mean to hurt you. There are so many well-meaning people who unintentionally hurt children, thinking they are doing the right thing for them. Your camp counselor devoted her life to helping children; but on this day, she got it very, very wrong." He looked intently at Ten. "I'm sad that happened to you." Then, standing in front of her, he held her face in his hands, and kissed her on the forehead.

The world seemed to stop spinning as Ten and Jesus gazed

into each other's eyes. The entire porch breathed a deep, collective sigh. Cricket songs filled the air in a celebration chorus. This time, crickets meant more than silence. Jesus not only listened; he understood and loved them.

SALVATION WITHOUT RELATIONSHIP

It was a lot to absorb. As I sat thinking, I just assumed Jesus had left the porch. But that's ridiculous. Jesus doesn't leave us.

Suddenly I was the one sitting on the swing, and Jesus now sat across from *me*. Though aware of all the parts inside of me, it was my sixty-six-year-old eyes that were now held by the eyes of Jesus—maybe for the very first time ever; certainly, the first time since I was ten. I felt much like a ten-year-old child as I said, "Jesus, I never understood why I didn't feel any different after asking you to forgive me and come into my heart. I now understand there was nothing to forgive. But if you came into my heart, why didn't I feel different?"

Jesus may have rolled his eyes, but I can't vouch for that.

"Those weren't my words," he began. "You know them from songs, prayers, and preaching. I talked a lot about the heart but didn't say those words. The intent was to believe and walk in relationship. Asking me to come into your heart confused you and made it about something other than the relationship I desired for you. There wasn't ever a time when I wasn't there."

"That makes sense." I laughed, recalling a memory. "One time, a friend's little girl asked if the peas she was eating for dinner were going into her heart along with Jesus. That's just one example of how these things can confuse children."

Jesus and I both laughed as we shook our heads.

Then his expression saddened. "How could you possibly have felt any different? You were forced to say you were sorry for something you didn't do. You told the truth but were accused of lying. It wasn't right to ask you to keep the secret in the first place, but your dad was doing the best he could to protect you from what others might think and say if they knew the truth. Then the camp counselor flinched, rejected your true story, and created more shame. You had no choice in these things. And it did feel worse."

"Yes, it felt worse," I responded. "I see now, going through the motions because of fear, prevented me from feeling you there. There was no comfort, only a sense that I had done something so horrible that even God had abandoned me."

Jesus leaned back and sighed. "That is exactly how everyone feels who comes to me by being shamed. It was so difficult for you to see yourself as I saw you. There was never anything wrong with you. You were a precious creation intended to grow up and walk through your life with me. You were born for relationships with people and God, but you could never trust. You have amazed me by staying true to who you are no matter what happened to you."

The others had gathered closer. Some of them—teens, young adults, and adults—also had made trauma-driven choices that the church would call sin. They had unwound many layers of shame from around those choices and understood how truly powerless and vulnerable they had been. Now, watching Jesus talk to Ten, they felt robbed of the walk through life with him that God had intended.

Non Janyne spoke for the others. "Jesus, our shame kept us at a distance from you. We spent our adult life controlling what we believed was our 'sinful nature.' The trauma and shame kept us from enjoying a relationship, but we never turned away."

"No, you never did." Jesus smiled. "And you are not alone. Painful childhood experiences inform many who are doing their best to walk with me. They will find themselves in the pages you write. They need to know they are not alone. They need to know I have always loved them."

Ten was listening. She leaned toward Non Janyne and said, "Our readers may not have the exact same story as me, but they have one of their own. What happened to me was important to the story, wasn't it?"

"Oh my, yes," Non Janyne said. "Without understanding your camp story, it was impossible to ever explain why we couldn't access the abundant life. We could never reach the Emerald City without you."

'We must journey on until we find the road of yellow brick again,' said Dorothy, 'and then we can keep on to the Emerald City.'

−Oz

The occupants of the porch fell into a reflective silence as the last rays of sunlight vanished below the tree line. The evening felt cooler and the Comforter busied herself lighting candles and covering children with additional cozy blankets.

Eventually Non Janyne cleared her throat. "Well, that was certainly an unexpected detour."

"A necessary one. I'm not sure I'd call it a detour," Jane responded. "We needed to know how this sad memory kept us from the abundant life."

"Yes!" Janyne exclaimed exuberantly. "What a mistake to leave out the children! We need the children!"

The children all giggled, glad Janyne had remembered them.

Then, they all heard the laughter that had confused them earlier.

Ten grinned, "Oh! It's Jesus! We just didn't see him then; but he is always with us."

Non Janyne, suddenly overtaken by the humor of it all, laughed so hard she began hiccuping. The Comforter dashed into the kitchen for a cup of water, and the children tried to scare the hiccups out of her.

(Jesus and I smiled at each other. Non Janyne was becoming more fully human all the time.)

At this exact moment, Dorothy returned from her search for the Yellow Brick Road and looked a bit confused as everyone tried to help Non Janyne. Noticing all the laughing faces, though, Dorothy said, "It seems the evening has gone well for everyone.... The Yellow Brick Road is not far away now, but we should probably rest here on the porch until morning."

Everyone agreed, Non Janyne finally stopped hiccuping, the children began yawning, and the adults grabbed more cozy blankets for themselves. Then, feeling they now had a better understanding of the book to be written and the story to be told, the three adult selves found spots to settle down for the night. It would be a long journey to the Emerald City, but finally the abundant life seemed possible. Tomorrow the Yellow Brick Road would guide them to their first stop—California. A long life lay ahead of them to recount. A long, brave life.

PART I
CALIFORNIA

'It is a long way to the Emerald City, and it will take you many days. The country here is rich and pleasant, but you must pass through rough and dangerous places before you reach the end of your journey.'

—Oz

As she bustled around the porch, woke up the children, and folded the blankets, Dorothy was trying to figure out how to serve breakfast to so many people.

"Dorothy," I said. "There's really only one of us—well at the most only three adults—and they take care of the children. We can all just be 'me' as we travel. You know, 'adult me.' The children can step in if they need to, but it's really just me—or us three."

Dorothy looked relieved. "It gets confusing sometimes. But yes, that would make things easier. One mouth to feed (or three) is much more manageable! We won't have much food along the Yellow Brick Road."

I laughed and suggested Non Janyne introduce Part I while we ate breakfast. Dorothy agreed.

Non Janyne put her hands on the keyboard.

⁓

The following three chapters tell the story of my young-adult life after college and before moving to Missouri. The story is based on memories and recent processing I have done about my life. I did no writing during those young adult years; no journals (something avoided at all costs my entire life); no poems (written during my college years but destroyed just before therapy began), and no short stories. There were no e-mails (that was way before e-mail), or letters (written in copious numbers before and during college), or notated calendars (kept up until this time) that survived. The glaring fact is, I didn't hold on to any form of personal writing. The fear of revealing something that someone might read, blocked the writing that could have brought healing.

～

Out of the corner of my eye I saw Dorothy tapping her elegantly-clad foot. The introductory material had taken too long. Breakfast had ended long ago. So, to move things along, she quoted from Oz.

'It seems to me I can scarcely wait till I get to Oz, and you must admit this is a very long journey.'
–Oz

Laughing, I agreed. "Yes, we need to keep moving if we plan to ever reach the Emerald City!"

But despite Dorothy's impatience, a few things needed explaining before Chapter One could begin.

"Dorothy, now that the story of my life begins in earnest, you can help the readers keep things straight. Sometimes it will be important to mix the 'now' of the story as it is being told, with my more recent understandings. Then, some things need to be told together even if they didn't happen at the same time. Healing wasn't a straight line."

"Yes," Dorothy agreed. "In my story, *The Wizard of Oz*, the Yellow Brick Road feels like a straight path, but it certainly wasn't straight."

"Exactly! We should also watch for missing details to help those who have not read my story in *BRAVE*, though my readers should stop here and read Addendum I: A Synopsis of *BRAVE*, before continuing."

"Oh, agreed," Dorothy said. "It sounds like a lot of things to accomplish and keep straight, but let's remain optimistic!"

I smiled at Dorothy, confident of the help this positive-thinking child would provide.

> 'Where are you all going?'
> 'To the Emerald City,' said Dorothy.
> 'To see the Great Oz.'
> 'Oh, indeed!' exclaimed the man. 'Are you sure that Oz will see you?'
> 'Why not?' she replied.
>
> —Oz

1
CALIFORNIA DREAMS

*Then, being prepared for the journey, they all started for the
Emerald City; and the Winkies gave them three cheers and
many good wishes to carry with them.*

–Oz

With college finished, and diploma in hand, my optimistic
young-adult self left the ocean view behind and headed
to Sacramento. Like Dorothy setting out for the Emerald City,
I embarked from college believing it would be possible to find
a way to a happier future. Also, like Dorothy, I was naïve about
the dangers. Dangers existed in the world, and inner turmoil
also presented danger. The optimism of young adulthood persuaded me that I could leave the past behind. Alas, this is not
feasible without healing.

Family connections secured a job as an assistant director at
a church preschool and my brother and I would share a house
owned by our parents. This all seemed like a great post-college
plan—until it wasn't.

The director of the school became an instant friend, and
this made life enjoyable, except that my idealistic college-grad-
uate self quickly had her expectations dashed. Churches sometimes open preschools under the guise (and maybe the intent)
of ministry, but they pay bills by absorbing the tuition. While
this church paid employees an adequate wage (not generally the
case with preschools), the supplies and equipment for the children were either non existent or in ill repair.

The job required church membership. But after seeing how
little the church invested in the preschool, my idealistic self

refused to join. The day I resigned and explained the need to leave in one week instead of giving the normal two-week notice, the recently-hired church administrator (drawing a salary from the preschool) said, "Well, go ahead. It doesn't matter a hill of beans if you're here or not."

It probably didn't. They could hire someone else for less than they had agreed to pay a college graduate. As this administrator kept his focus on the paperwork in front of him, I gathered myself and left.

The choice to seek another job had involved both personal and professional reasons. While living in Sacramento enabled me to enjoy time spent with my dad, the four years at college had provided independence from my mother. Returning to our tense relationship proved challenging. In addition, the idealistic, starry-eyed desire to do something important probably wasn't going to materialize at this first after-college job. Besides, the ocean called!

The plan? Use my two-week vacation to go job hunting in southern California. Several "coincidences" occurred during the trip, along with a "God prompting"[8] that led to a new job.

A friend lived in Huntington Beach, and so it made sense to hunt for a school in the area where she worked. One school seemed like a possibility, but anxiety kept me driving right on by. However, the "God prompting" to turn the car around and go back felt so clear. I did, and in a matter of days, a job as the preschool director became mine. This newly-accepted position would change my life in many ways.

---

8. The term "God prompting" indicates an invitation to the good that God wished to bring to my life. This does not mean a choice to not follow this prompting would have placed me outside of God's will, but I would have missed out on the blessings brought by following the prompt.

A NEW LIFE

Landing a job as a preschool director proved to be a great start to a new life. The preschool had an enrollment of over one hundred, and a daily average attendance of around eighty. This level of responsibility required a huge leap in leadership skills for someone just a year out of college; especially when the employees (all but one) were older than I. My inexperience made lots of beginner mistakes; but the school flourished.

Relationships with the staff were a mixture of building friendships, establishing authority, advocating for higher wages, and building a pleasant school and work environment. Learning to establish professional boundaries for myself while caring for employees proved challenging. This process included successful interactions and a few epic failures. Despite the challenges, memories from those years include laughter, loving the small children in our care, and building a reputation as a quality school.

Some of the same church-preschool issues existed, but now as part of a larger school (pre-kindergarten to grade twelve) it was easier to navigate … most of the time.

FRIENDSHIP AND AWKWARD SITUATIONS

This new life included an abundance of friendships and an active young adult group at the church—most of whom held positions in the school. Memories of those years include choir practices, volleyball games, sitting by the apartment pool on Sunday afternoons, walking on the beach, playing with a friend's baby girl, shopping, and enjoying restaurants. There were so many friends and so much laughter.

During the first few weeks at the school, several high school staff members would see me and tell me to "Go back to class." My appearance, much like a sixteen-year-old with long blonde hair, somehow wasn't commanding respect. One prospective parent enrolling her child in the school even asked me, "What are the qualifications for a director?" Fair enough.

My uncanny ability to move from one awkward situation to another only added to the "blonde image." These situations were sometimes (but not always) a result of not being fully present or grounded. Walking right into mirrors in department stores occurred often. Self-deprecating humor became a survival skill.

Sometimes storytelling acted as a cover for dissociative episodes that required damage control, but other times life simply provided a funny story. So many odd things happened that the awkward dissociative episodes just got mixed in and didn't appear unusual.

There were endless stories.

One day while out to lunch with work friends, the belt on my wrap-around skirt broke and we all dug in our purses and came up with a paperclip to hold me together. Another day, a plastic-coated menu melted as I held it over the candle. The growing circle of melting plastic mesmerized me!

Then, while navigating the bank drive-through, the canister slipped, fell, and rolled directly under my car. Moving forward (carefully) while waving wildly at the car behind mine, took two attempts before retrieving the canister.

The awkward moments were unending. Right after Thanksgiving, while driving down the alley to my apartment, a turkey bone impaled a car tire. I quickly drove to the tire store and approached the young man at the counter.

"There is a turkey bone in my tire."

(Silence)

"Just a minute," he said and walked back into the garage area. Gathering a group of mechanics, he pointed at me and laughed.

Rounding the counter and ignoring the "Staff Only" signs, I joined the group of laughing mechanics. "It *is* a turkey bone," I insisted. "Come look at the tire."

Marching out of the shop like a mother duck leading her ducklings, I walked to the car and pointed at the now-flat tire. They stared at the tire, then at me, then at the tire, and then at me again.

Finally, one of them spoke up. "It appears to be a turkey bone."

"Yes." I glared at him, giving my long-blonde hair a toss. "It is a turkey bone and that is a road hazard the insurance will cover."

They all agreed.

~

Dorothy giggled. "Toto would have loved to have that turkey bone. You really did have strange things happen to you, didn't you?"

"Yes," I answered. "This has always been true. I'm glad, because laughter provided the best medicine. No matter what bad things happened, many other things brought laughter. Nothing felt better than a good hearty laugh."

"Agreed," Dorothy said. "Laughter makes even tough times much easier to endure."

The sun shone brightly as our friends turned their faces toward the Land of the South. They were all in the best of spirits, and laughed and chatted together.

–Oz

2
CALIFORNIA NIGHTMARE

'You have plenty of courage, I am sure,' answered Oz. 'All you need is confidence in yourself. There is no living thing that is not afraid when it faces danger. The True courage is in facing danger when you are afraid, and that kind of courage you have in plenty.'

–Oz

The two young adults were discussing the previous chapter. Jane said, "Janyne, you were so strong. You just went on vacation and found a new job—just like that. As if it were simple. I guess things *were* simple for you. You were brave."

"I can see why you think this is true," her twin said. "But *you* were holding all the pain. There is no bravery bigger than living with so much pain. Everyone saw me on the outside, but you had a different story. I think you should write this chapter. You survived. You were afraid, but you still survived."

"OK," Jane said. "I see your point. Thank you. This chapter will somewhat repeat a chapter in *BRAVE*, but it's important to fully tell what happened in this book also. Though we might want to give a trigger warning.[9] It's a painful story."

---

9. Trigger warning: In this section, some of the details leading up to and including a suicide attempt at twenty-three may be triggering. I am sensitive to this and have tried to give essential information without excessive descriptive content. Suicidal ideation is a common struggle for trauma survivors. See Addendum IV, Suicide Prevention Resources, and seek help if struggling. National Suicide Prevention Lifeline: Call 1-800-273-8255

"Good idea, Jane. You always think of others. You will be careful as you tell it."

UNEXPLAINABLE THINGS

This new life overflowed with good memories. It was almost perfect. But entanglements from the past kept reappearing. Sadly, within a few months, someone surfaced and brought more pain with him. No one in my life knew about one heartbreaking day, when I drove alone up a mountain road and attempted to drive over the edge of a cliff. It was one horrible day in a new life filled with many good days—and it could have ended tragically.

I, myself, retained only vague memories of that painful day—fragmented sensations and odd occurrences that defied explanation. Until many years later, when I processed the repressed memories during EMDR therapy, several things in my life made little sense.

First unexplainable thing: An overpowering fear of mountain roads. While on a trip through Colorado, this consuming fear became apparent. Though I was never crazy about mountain roads, this pathological, nauseating fear felt so much worse.

Second unexplainable thing: A sudden onset of nightmares about car brakes failing while careening towards a cliff. The dream always ended just before the car went over the edge.

Third unexplainable thing: A parking brake that became so loose it was undependable on hills. Eventually, while we were dating, Scott noticed the problem and asked if I had ever driven with the emergency brake pulled.

No, not that I could remember.

Fourth unexplainable thing: A dress that I loved went missing. How odd. Sometime later, I purchased another one like it. Eventually, the two dresses seemed to merge into one in my memory. They weren't the same, though; a dress had vanished.

Fifth unexplainable thing: And finally, a few years later, while preparing to sell the car, I looked for a letter I had hidden under the mat in the trunk of the car, and it had vanished. When I thought about it, I had a vague sense of it ending up in a roadside trash bin.

Nothing connected these fragments together, though—not until therapy forty years later. I did have a vague sense of inner struggles and a need to hide them from everyone. Living life at two levels was a well-practiced expertise. Secrets needed keeping and life went on.

REMEMBERING TRAUMA

During the third year of therapy, fragmented memories of an attempted suicide began to surface. While I processed these memories, flashes of insight clarified many pieces that had never made sense. Trauma will fragment memories; but during healing, the mind begins to connect the dots between the fragments. The ability to tell a sequential narrative is a sign of healing.

The story of my suicide attempt at the edge of a cliff was first published as a guest essay and then included in *BRAVE*.[10] That version of the story did not provide many details. The following additional details demonstrate how hard my subconscious worked to protect me from the truth of what occurred.

My drive to the cliff began after being raped.

Dissociative coping strategies helped me as a child, but the

---

10. The cliff experience was originally published as a guest essay on the blog "Uncontrolling Love." It may be accessed at http://uncontrollinglove.com/ 2016/11/10/when-god-is-not-in-control/. The essay has since been published in the book compilation, *Uncontrolling Love: Conversations on the Love of God*, edited by Thomas Jay Oord (SacraSage Press, 2017).

same strategies put me in jeopardy as an adult. Lawyers portraying victims as complicit is one reason why many women never report rapes. Understanding the effects of trauma is essential for helping rape victims. My freeze response to the unwanted advances caused me to appear complicit—even to myself.

At twenty three, it was possible for me to get out of the situation; but I froze and dissociated. I only retained a fragment of the memory, ending with an unwanted advance but leaving out the rape. Many years later, during EMDR (Eye Movement Desensitization and Reprocessing[11]) therapy, my body seemed to float near the ceiling and merely watch what happened next. This dissociative episode enabled me to not consciously remember, but the subconscious explosion of fear and shame sent me up a mountain road with a plan to end the unbearable pain.

WANTING MY PAIN TO END

My car left the freeway at an exit leading to a winding mountain road. Stopping at a roadside picnic area, I retrieved a letter from the trunk of the car and threw it in the trash bin before continuing. The letter could not be in the trunk when they found my car.

A hairpin curve loomed ahead as my car picked up speed, left the asphalt, and began skidding across the gravel. I was on my way to my death, but at the last moment, my foot began searching for the brake pedal. It found the clutch instead. In desperation I pulled up on the parking brake. The car skidded to a stop.

---

11. Both professional and client-oriented information about EMDR are available at EMDR Institute, Inc. http://www.emdr.com/

Jumping from the car, I ran to the edge of the cliff screaming, "I didn't die! I didn't die!" My emotions were a mixture of relief and a sense of failure. As I stopped just short of the edge, I became aware of a man climbing over the barrier....

"No! Please don't rape me!" I cried.

The man, who had seen my car careening toward the cliff, immediately backed away and began speaking in a calm, steady voice.

"Do you know where you are standing?"

"Yes. But I can float. I'm safe. I can float."

(While processing this memory with EMDR, the world became still—as my body gently swayed in what seemed like water. The only sound was a consistent *whoosh, whoosh, whoosh,* as of blood rushing through an umbilical cord. My troubled mind had returned to the safety of the womb. It felt completely peaceful; my body seemed to float in the air.)

As the man kept calmly talking, the truth finally sank in that my feet were at the edge of a cliff. I wanted to end the pain; but I didn't necessarily want to die. As I attempted to turn and step back, the ground crumbled, and I slid over the edge with my face scraping against the rocky edge of the cliff. Frantic, I grabbed a tree root, my hands gripping in desperation as the man rushed to pull me back up over the edge.

Lying on the ground in my torn dress, it felt as if small children were clinging and crawling on me (much as they do in Storyteller figurines[12]). My dissociated child selves were terrified—I had almost killed them.

Many years later, while sitting on the therapy couch, this

---

12. Storyteller Dolls are clay figurines crafted by the Pueblo people of New Mexico. The adult figures are usually surrounded by listening children who climb on the Storyteller or sit on his/her shoulders or lap.

truth came to life when my therapist suggested that adult Janyne could care for the child self who wasn't feeling safe.

"No, she can't," my child self said. "She almost killed us. We don't trust her." She made a valid point.

How could they trust me? This traumatic memory needed reframing. Wrapping all my child selves in a warm Navajo blanket reminiscent of my New Mexico childhood, we acknowledged our fear. The trauma continued to release for days while I shook under piles of blankets. Holding my child selves close, I understood it would be some time before they fully trusted me. Their trust in me had been destroyed at the cliff.

I couldn't trust myself.

PROCESSING TRAUMA

While processing the memory, I felt myself pull up on the emergency brake and attempt to turn from the cliff. No matter what happened, part of me always wanted to live. There is no possible way to describe the inner turmoil at the edge of the cliff. All the pain that took years of therapy to heal, was completely present. My deepest compassion goes to those who find themselves in similar unbearable circumstances.

My rescuer saved my life but had few options for keeping me safe. Getting in a stranger's car and leaving mine behind wasn't a possibility I could entertain; so we agreed that I would follow him. He drove slowly. As I concentrated on following him, a dissociative fog enabled me to "forget" things too excruciating to consciously remember. By the time the freeway became visible, I didn't know why I was following such a slow car; it made no sense to me. The stranger in the slow car watched as I passed and headed my car to the freeway.

Arriving back at my apartment, I began tearing up a stack of letters which once felt like friendship, but now cried betrayal. It seemed to help. The pile of hundreds of tiny pieces grew in the trash can. My tendency to obsessively tear paper in times of stress finally makes sense, as does the letter missing from my trunk, the non-functional brake, the nightmares, the fear of mountain roads, and the missing dress (thrown in the dumpster along with all the torn paper).

The terror of the cliff experience added an entirely new level of distrust—mostly of myself. I needed to somehow get back down the mountain and act like nothing ever happened. The dissociative ability to "forget" was a powerful skill set by this time.

While not consciously remembering what happened at the cliff, my subconscious never forgot. I drove my car from the darkness of betrayal to a false light of dissociation that would control my life for the next forty years. Though my subconscious repressed the memory, the emotions and feelings associated with both the rape and suicide attempt were often triggered by parking brakes, mountain roads, and driving on gravel.

Non Janyne, who emerged on the way down the mountain road, enabled me to make many good life decisions, but not always in healthy ways. Her greatest desire? To be "normal!" The need and determination to appear normal drove my life.

The effects of this one traumatic day included many classic symptoms of Post-Traumatic Stress Disorder (PTSD)[13]. So much of my anxiety, panic attacks, phobias, and depression discussed in Part II grew out of this traumatic experience subconsciously relegated to the graveyard of horrible memories.

---

13. PTSD symptoms included flashbacks (reliving) and reenactments, dreams/nightmares, frightening thoughts (including recurring suicidal thoughts), avoidance of places, objects, and feelings; emotional outbursts, anxiety, and being easily startled. For a full overview from the National Institute of Mental Health, see: https://www.nimh.nih.gov/health/topics/post-traumatic-stress-disorder-ptsd/index.shtml

It was the unknowing knowing of trauma. Would it have been better to remember or not remember? Difficult to say. But either way, processing what occurred wasn't possible.

Then, forty years later, in therapy my processing brought clarity to the events and established my role as that of an innocent victim. Shame always tells the lie of somehow being responsible for the evil choices of others. Holding this shame as my own, layered on top of Ten's camp experience—only confirmed (to me) my sinful identity. Any mention of sin took me back to my partial memory of this day—a partial memory for which I repeatedly asked God for forgiveness.

In traditions that view the recounting of our own responsibility/sin as a path for growth, we often further embed shame for those things that were done to us but that we mistakenly believe we caused. This is especially true of childhood abuse. This builds an internalized message of responsibility: "It was my fault." This false belief then becomes the lens through which we view all future experiences.

In hindsight, I now see that dissociation was a gift from God. It didn't bring healing, but it got me down the mountain and enabled me to continue with life as if that day had never happened. On the surface, a terrific plan!

~

Dorothy, who had listened intently as Jane told her painful story, said, "Knowing each other's stories is very important. That's how I understood there wasn't any reason to be afraid of the Winged Monkeys."

'That is a long story,' answered the King, with a winged laugh; 'but as we have a long journey before us, I will pass the time by telling you about it, if you wish.'
'I shall be glad to hear it,' [Dorothy] replied.
−Oz

"Exactly," I said. "Your willingness to hear the Winged Monkeys' story changed everything. You realized what they did wasn't their fault. It's important for us to understand our own and others' stories. Thank you for listening to mine."

"You're welcome," Dorothy replied. "I listened to the Scarecrow, Lion, and Tin Man's stories too. Their stories made me sad but also helped me understand why each one wanted to go to the Emerald City. Now I understand why you are traveling on your own Yellow Brick Road."

They all started upon the journey, greatly enjoying the walk through the soft, fresh grass; and it was not long before they reached the road of yellow brick and turned again toward the Emerald City where the Great Oz dwelt.

–Oz

3
THE SEARCH FOR NORMAL

'It must be inconvenient to be made of flesh,' said the Scarecrow thoughtfully, 'for you must sleep, and eat and drink. However, you have brains, and it is worth a lot of bother to be able to think properly.'

–Oz

Before beginning this new chapter, Dorothy wanted to ask a question. "You needed to be able to think properly when you came down the mountain. Thinking was Non Janyne's job, right?"

"Why yes," Jane answered. "I hadn't thought of it that way, but I held all the emotional pain and certainly struggled with thinking clearly. Janyne hurt physically and couldn't think. We needed someone to think clearly."

Non Janyne smiled. "I never had a problem thinking."

Jane and Janyne giggled. Non Janyne did have a tendency to think highly of herself. Dorothy laughed with them. It reminded her of the conversation between Glinda and the Scarecrow.

'I will return to the Emerald City,' [the Scarecrow] replied, 'for Oz has made me its ruler and the people like me....'
'I shall command the Winged Monkeys to carry you to the gates of the Emerald City,' said Glinda, 'for it would be a shame to deprive the people of so wonderful a ruler.'
'Am I really wonderful?' asked the Scarecrow.
'You are unusual,' replied Glinda.

–Oz

Non Janyne rolled her eyes. "Well, I did know exactly what we needed to do when we came down the mountain. We needed to look normal.... Maybe I should tell this chapter."

They all agreed to this. But Janyne smirked and said, "As long as you don't try to be stellar. You do have that tendency."

SEARCHING FOR MR. RIGHT

"Normal" meant different things at various times; at this point in my life, marriage topped the looking-normal list. My friends were getting married one after another. Surely nothing could be more normal than marriage.

Fulfilling the goal of marriage is problematic unless one dates. For good reasons, dating didn't show up on my list of enjoyable activities; but being normal required it. So, I went on a few dates—all nice guys, but not Mr. Right.

What would Mr. Right be like? The answer wasn't clear, but for me protection seemed important, especially since perpetrators had decimated my conceptual understanding of love. In addition, attachment issues made it easy to confuse attachment needs with love. There probably wasn't much of anything "normal" about my desire to marry.

Meanwhile, my friends getting married were undoubtedly more typical. They were falling in love and getting married. That made sense. The process seemed simple. So, the hunt began.

My group of friends fluctuated between girlish giggles about the possibilities of Mr. Right, to more mature considerations about the kind of person with whom we wanted to spend the rest of our lives. Dreaming about weddings, and perusing the pages of *Brides* magazine, made me feel so normal!

Good looking seemed like an important attribute for Mr. Right. My friends and I spotted a potential candidate visiting our church and tried to learn his name. But he was elusive!

This potential Mr. Right carried a large leather Bible with him every week, and we thought perhaps his name was embossed on the cover. One Sunday morning, settling into the row behind him, we waited for the call to stand and sing. Then leaning forward as one, we peered down at the Bible.

The embossed words read, "Genuine Leather." We collapsed into giggles.

We eventually learned his true identity, but we continued to refer to him as Genuine Leather. And no, he wasn't Mr. Right (though I don't remember why).

Another guy also seemed potentially promising. Happening by his office one day, I began chatting across the wide expanse of his meticulously polished mahogany desk. Prone to excessive saliva, as I spoke I spit a huge glob right in the middle of the shining glory of the desk—directly in front of him. He stared at it, while I searched for a tissue and mentally crossed him off my list. Anyone who couldn't laugh with me about my continuous stream of awkward moments couldn't be Mr. Right.

The hunt wasn't going well. I almost made a bad choice; but my school administrator kindly but firmly admonished me and spoke wisdom into my life. Did his admonition trigger shame? Yes, that would be a given. But his nonjudgmental approach helped me to listen and make better choices.

As a young woman who desperately needed protection, poor choices were always a possibility. A small child deep inside me struggled with knowing who to trust, because those who should have proven trustworthy in the past, were not. Those young adult years could have turned disastrous without God's protection through the care and mentoring of friends.

～

Janyne and Jane were following along as Non Janyne wrote. Janyne smiled and said, "Not too bad, Non Janyne. Your story-telling is improving. Let's see how you do on the next section. We can tell you really wanted to start analyzing but stopped yourself."

Non Janyne smiled in appreciation and continued.

THOSE BLUE EYES

One of my coworkers introduced me to her daughter who had just graduated from college and returned home. She thought her daughter and I would be great friends. She was right.

Kay (who would eventually share the name McConnaughey and design the *BRAVE* book covers) said to me, "I want you to meet Scott. He is Brad's brother. When Brad comes home from college, maybe we could go on a double date."

The next Sunday, I found Scott and Kay sitting together. When she introduced us, I looked at his blue eyes and was immediately mesmerized ... until I noticed his Hang Ten™ shorts, T-shirt, Docksiders™ ... and ... no socks.

⌒

Janyne interrupted: "His not wearing socks was almost a game ender for you, Non Janyne. But those eyes! I was the one who noticed the eyes.... Sorry, had to say that. Now go ahead."

Non Janyne agreed about the shorts and lack of socks in church, but then continued writing.

⌒

My conservative upbringing would bump up against this beach bum husband of mine our entire marriage; but on that day, his blue eyes captivated me. It might be possible to ignore the lack of socks for the time being, I thought, since I did feel safe standing next to him. His stature and strength would surely provide protection.

⌒

This time Jane interrupted: "I was the one who wanted protection!"

"Well, yes, you were," Janyne agreed. "And I needed to know he wouldn't be boring."

Non Janyne, who thought boring was fine, rolled her eyes. Then she continued.

～

A church banquet became our first "date" (we never had an actual date). We arrived in the slowly-filling room and saw no one we knew. Sitting alone at a large round table, we began to feel uncomfortable when no one chose to join us.

To fill the air space, I spoke. "It appears no one wants to sit here. We may have the table to ourselves."

And with that, we spontaneously started creating table companions, introducing them to each other, and initiating conversations around the table. Eventually the room filled, and people joined our table, but we were not nearly as enamored with these intruders as we were with our imaginary companions.

～

Janyne giggled. "I was pleasantly surprised, too, when Scott started making up people!"

THE FIRST KISS AND PROPOSAL

Scott and I became best friends—just what we both needed. My intuition about him being a protector proved true; no one could have protected me any better.

As our relationship became more serious, he sensed my feelings—those of a skittish rabbit ready to bolt for cover if frightened. To some extent, this actually described both of us. It took many conversations and walks along the beach before we trusted each other. We were talking about home-decorating colors long before we discussed marriage. That felt safer. By the time he finally kissed me, I had begun to wonder if it would ever happen.

～

"That was me again," Janyne grinned brightly. "OK, keep going, Non Janyne."

Non Janyne continued, even though all the interruptions were beginning to distract her. (That would happen a lot over the years!)

~

Speaking of the first kiss, what happened next should have forewarned us about what our future might be like....

Head lice!

I had to drive to Scott's work and inform him about my itchy, crawly head—and check his head. He worked at the same optical shop as his mother (whom I had not previously met). Scott remained calm. We never told her about the head lice. We agreed that some things are better left unsaid.

We walked through the awkwardness but couldn't get rid of the head lice. I shampooed, combed, bagged clothes, fumigated the preschool, ironed my mattress, and still—for seven long weeks—kept finding head lice. So exhausting!

One day a preschool staff member offered me a taste of her soda. I made the mistake of taking a sip. And then I came down with mono! I felt like the Egyptian plagues had found me. Through it all, Scott proved he would consistently take care of me.

And, along the way, we stumbled into an engagement.

"How many children do you want?" Scott asked.

"Isn't this a bit premature to ask since you haven't even asked me to marry you?"

Not easily trapped, he replied, "What would you say if I did?"

To which I said, "You will have to ask me and find out."

"Will you?"

This was getting painful.

"Will I what?" I asked.

"Marry me."

Still not there.

"Ask me. You need to ask me!"

"Will you marry me?"

"Yes!"

～

Jane shook her head. "Non Janyne, you weren't letting go without a definite proposal, were you?"

Janyne laughed. "No she wasn't."

Non Janyne looked at the other two. "Well, it wouldn't have been normal to up and marry without a proper proposal. But planning a wedding would prove even more problematic."

"True," Janyne said. "Everything went so well ... you know ... until it didn't. That's usually how things go."

Dorothy nodded in agreement. "It was like that in Oz, too. Everything moved along fine until trouble appeared."

> *'What is your trouble?' asked the Lion quietly.*
> *'We are all threatened,' answered the tiger, 'by a fierce*
> *enemy which has lately come into this forest.'*
> —Oz

4
A ROUGH ROAD TO MARRIAGE

It was difficult to walk without falling into muddy holes, for the grass was so thick that it hid them from sight. However, by carefully picking their way, they got safely along until they reached solid ground.

—Oz

Dorothy was reviewing the notes that Non Janyne had jotted down for this chapter. "Wow, you were trying to plan a wedding and things just kept going wrong!"

Jane sighed. "Yes, it felt that way. It was a rough road, kind of like what happened after you climbed over the wall into the china country. We tried to tread carefully, but everything we did just made it worse."

"Yes!" Dorothy said. "We were trying to be so cautious but still broke the cow's leg and the church!"

"But that wasn't too bad considering how brittle everything was," Jane said. "For us it didn't seem to matter how careful we were.... But I do think Non Janyne is the one to tell the story."

"Yes, Non Janyne, please continue," said Dorothy. "We need to get you to the wedding. It will be as great a relief as getting us out of the china country was!"

FROM MONO TO FIRING

Barely recovering from mono, I returned to work; and the newly-hired church administrator fired me the next week. It wasn't just one episode of "Humans Behaving Badly," it was an entire season.

While not claiming complete innocence in all the drama,

for the most part I wasn't at fault and my actions were misunderstood. My survival strategies (specifically, being overly honest to try to avoid conflict) interacted with their need to control me. In working with survivors, trying to exercise control over them is always the worst strategy.

"Yes," Jane confessed. "I was the one who tried to be too honest. I just kept trying to explain things. I am much better about that now."

Non Janyne, who had consistently found herself doing damage control in these situations, thanked Jane for accepting responsibility, then continued.

~

It all began when the church decided to move the preschool students in with the elementary school day care on Wednesday nights at five o'clock, so visitation dinner could be set up. As simple as this seemed to them, it wasn't a viable solution because of state licensing regulations. Children from our licensed preschool couldn't be combined with the unlicensed day care children. Explaining and providing documentation didn't help prove my point.

In the conflict over this, I saw the writing on the wall. I knew it was time to leave. So when they fired me, I had already located a job teaching kindergarten in a nearby city. But the new job wouldn't start for three months.

All my attempts to smooth things over just made the church administrator angrier. Finally, he summoned me to his office and handed me a paycheck for time worked. He told me he would personally make sure no one else ever hired me to work at a church or school again.

~

Non Janyne paused. "I worked hard; enrollment was up; they knew I planned to leave; and they gave no legitimate cause for firing me. It made no sense."

"I agree," Janyne said. "We will never understand. Sometimes my independence rubbed bosses the wrong way, though."

"Well, I did try to enforce the state regulations. It seemed important." Non Janyne always wondered why they didn't want her to comply with the regulations.

"Yes,' Jane added. "But no matter what, he didn't need to tell our friends not to come to our wedding shower. That crossed a line."

True, many things crossed a line.

Non Janyne did feel sad for Jane who suffered the most during conflicts. "This wasn't the only time this type of thing occurred. We might need to pause our storytelling, for a bit, to explain why."

Both Janyne and Jane knew what Non Janyne planned to say—and agreed it needed saying. The story on the surface didn't explain the subconscious effects of trauma which constantly drove my interactions in times of conflict.

Jane sighed. "It always felt like everything became a fight for our very life, and my reactions were often perceived as a lack of respect for authority. It was challenging to prepare for our wedding amid the conflict. You should explain how our story kept getting us caught up in these situations."

Non Janyne was eager. This was another opportunity to analyze!

FLASHES OF INSIGHT

It wasn't clear why conflicts with those in power (predominantly, but not always, men) seemed so common. During therapy, pieces of this puzzle (though slow to resolve) came in flashes of insight—five of them, to be exact.

First, my experiences of powerlessness as a child played out in my authority relationships as an adult. From childhood on, it was difficult for me to respect those in similar positions to the adults who should have provided protection to me as a child, but did not. This was problematic.

Second, the church, ever-present in my life as a child, did not always feel safe. While many in the church loved me and cared about me, there was an underbelly to the church that kept me on guard.

Third, as a young adult I had an experience where my seeking help resulted in betrayal. I learned that leaders often have feet of clay. This made it impossible for me to respect position. Leaders needed to demonstrate something greater than a title to earn my trust.

Fourth, my natural desire to lead, along with strong leadership skills, made conflicts almost certain, especially with ultra-conservative religious men in positions of authority. Choosing to spend my entire life in settings where patriarchy was the predominant leadership structure (even within my denominational heritage which ordains women) demonstrates the complete incongruence of trauma-based choices. It is common for abuse survivors to unwittingly reenact the trauma in both subtle and obvious ways.

Fifth, dissociative coping mechanisms provided the final nail in this coffin. While shifting flawlessly among adult selves, if triggered, any of my child selves might abruptly speak up. I would suddenly become a warrior, victim, careless teenager, or a small child filled with anxiety. Living as a small child in an adult body provided many mystifying moments for everyone.

TRUST AND BETRAYAL

Because my childhood abuse affected all developmental stages, I entered adulthood without achieving some important milestones—especially in the areas of trust, emotional regulation, and the understanding of self. Instead of jobs simply being a place of employment, I looked to the church and church-related schools to care for and protect me. As a pastor's child, this expectation seemed legitimate; but it resulted in my carrying unhealthy patterns over into adult life.

My powerlessness as a child created an unrealistic and unhealthy dependence on the church (and other people). It was difficult for me to separate from the settings where my abuse occurred, but also almost impossible for me to trust those in authority. This proved true throughout my life.

When I was fired, it made sense to be angry; but it felt more like betrayal at the deepest levels of my childhood pain. The church and church ministries had failed to protect me once again. My caregiver had been my abuser. This sense of betrayal created new layers around an already hurtful experience and placed me in the role of a powerless victim fighting for my life. It was difficult to lay the pain aside because it reinforced the incorrect and unbearable internalized childhood message of shame. Even actions which were clearly the responsibility of others, felt as if they were my fault.

~

Jane, appreciative of Non Janyne's insights, said, "Thank you for explaining all that. I really just wanted to feel safe."

Non Janyne understood. "Feeling safe doesn't come easy when early-childhood trauma has wired a person for hypervigilance. It is hard to ever feel safe, especially when the people in charge often make decisions based on the need to control instead of a willingness to listen.

Janyne, sensing that Non Janyne was starting down an analytical sidetrack, stepped in. "Anyone listening to our story in this chapter so far, can see that Scott and I kept getting sidetracked from the enjoyment of our engagement and the anticipation and preparations for our wedding." With an air of drama, she turned to Non Janyne, who sat at the typewriter. "But—there's more to the story!"

Non Janyne resumed typing.

ON THE WAY TO A WEDDING

Turmoil followed Scott and me all spring as we tried to prepare for our July wedding. A church staff member counseled Scott not to marry me (thankfully, he didn't listen). What he did do, was find another job and then resign from his job at the church.

Still weak from mono, it was not possible to find temporary employment, but I had to move out of my apartment. A friend graciously provided a place to stay. Then, because I was under contract, I tried to claim unpaid vacation pay and file a claim for wrongful termination. Sadly, I didn't have a copy of the signed contract. I was told that I hadn't signed it and it had subsequently and mysteriously vanished from the office.

My dad, along with a pastor friend who had previously been on staff at this church, tried to intervene on my behalf. But they finally both agreed it would only get worse if I continued to seek compensation; I wrote a letter to officially drop the claim.

Then, the message came—we could not have our wedding in the church sanctuary. What to do? My dad was the pastor of a church about eight hours away, so we immediately began long-distance wedding planning.

⁓

Jane leaned forward, "Such a mess! But Non Janyne, you were so good at finding solutions when these things happened. Thank you."

Janyne agreed and added, "Finding the wedding dress seemed like a miracle. It was on a sales rack for $75.00, and it fit perfectly!"

Jane smiled. "Yes. And then we found it featured in *Brides* magazine."

"That was God," the three said in one voice.

OUR WEDDING DAY

Our wedding day arrived as one of the hottest days of the year. My memories of the day are happy ones despite the fact that I only knew a few of my dad's kind church members who attended. We were grateful for our friends and family who had traveled to be there!

Jane looked across at Non Janyne, the wedding planner. "By choosing not to have a reception line, you helped us enjoy our wedding. Shaking hands would always trigger me, because of that terrible time when we were betrayed by a handshake."

"Yes," Janyne said. "Mother wasn't happy about not having a reception line. I couldn't have refused her. Non Janyne, you were strong, though!"

Non Janyne paused before moving on. "It wasn't clear why I felt so strongly about that. Now it makes sense as a subconscious trigger, but then it just felt like something I didn't like and decided it wouldn't be part of the wedding day. We didn't have all the understanding we have now."

No, we certainly didn't!

What a relief for Scott and me to finally overcome all the obstacles to becoming husband and wife. For our honeymoon, we travelled down the California coast on our way back home. Since most of the people we both knew, couldn't attend the wedding, close friends opened their home for a reception a week later. This took the sting out of having to change our wedding plans and provided an opportunity to gather with friends.

THE LIFE OF NEWLYWEDS

We settled into our little apartment and I began teaching kindergarten. We had already weathered enough trials to fill half a life together, but calamity continued to follow us. We faced an infestation of fleas from the previous renter and a queen bee got into the wall of our bathroom. Suddenly dozens of worker bees arrived as uninvited guests. Since Scott is allergic to bee stings, everything became extremely complicated.

But despite the fleas and bees, we were happy in our small apartment. Early in the morning I headed down the freeway to my teaching job, and I returned home after Scott had left for his optical job at a shopping mall.

On those afternoons, upon arriving home, I kept finding the pictures on the walls hanging crooked. Maybe the upstairs neighbors were dropping weights? It seemed possible. I didn't want to entertain the possibility of earth tremors in our earthquake-prone area. Whatever the reason, it became part of my routine to come home and straighten the pictures.

One Saturday, I noticed Scott trying to straighten the pictures. He said, "Every morning I find these are crooked."

"And they are crooked every day when I get home," I replied.

He stared at me for a second. Then he said, "Come here and straighten this picture."

So I did.

"You know you just made it crooked, right?"

"No, I just straightened it." Well, it looked straight to me!

"No, you just 'crookeded' it. We need to go see my dad (an optometrist) and get your eyes checked."

Glasses did help this particular problem. But I was to learn that, in many ways, my perspectives weren't like everyone else's. To this day, when asked if something is level, I just laugh. How would I know?

We were broke, but happy. Then Scott lost his job and we were even more broke—but still happy.

He began working at two jobs—a fast-food chicken restaurant and an aircraft plating company. He'd come home smelling like two kinds of grease. Yes, we were still happy—after he took a shower.

We each found someone strong enough to care for us and the years would prove the need was mutual. We found we could survive and make a life for ourselves.

And our life seldom had a dull moment.

～

"Good thing it wasn't dull," said Janyne. "I do dislike being bored."

"Well, it couldn't have been boring for long with you around," Non Janyne replied. Then thinking it might have sounded harsh, she continued. "Life required all three of us. I often wonder what it would have felt like to just be us and not to shift—though we didn't actually know we were shifting—but to remain focused or compassionate or fun-loving. We may be getting there, though.... I can even laugh now." And, indeed, she did laugh—not quite a Janyne laugh, but close.

"I can be more focused and compassionate," Janyne said.

"And I can now enjoy life while still experiencing difficult emotions," Jane said. "But these things weren't true of us when we began marriage with Scott."

Dorothy spotted her segue. "This book isn't about marriage, but you might want to say something about that before we move on."

Non Janyne agreed.

TAKING TRAUMA INTO MARRIAGE

Here's an interesting fact about marriage: The most common honeymoon destination is Disneyland or Disneyworld. All of us really are grown-up children searching for a forever friend. But enjoying Disneyland together and handling the stresses of every-day life are two very different things.

Most premarital counseling addresses normal stressors but not the effects of those entering marriage with multiple adverse childhood experiences. This was certainly true in 1979. We brought so much to our marriage without any form of premarital counseling after being denied access to marrying in the church we attended while dating (not that this counseling could have addressed our true needs, anyway).

We arrived at my dad's church the day before the wedding with nothing more than the turmoil of our engagement and lots of tenacity. In many ways, all the struggles created a formidable team. We seemed to sense that it would be us against the world more often than we wanted—certainly more often than we could understand.

Scott and I have talked about this in recent years as we have come to the other side of our healing journeys. We married as two friends, each believing the other would take care of them. We did the best we could and raised two remarkable children. We both consider this a miracle.

All the while, we hid in plain sight in the church. We met in the church, married in the church, and spent our lives ministering in the church. We appeared to be the perfect couple. Survival is often disguised as thriving.

Scott and I both wish we could have accessed professional help before marrying and starting a family—but certainly before reaching retirement age. We could have avoided so many struggles. We thought finding "normal" meant "falling in love." Even the music from our era told us love was enough.

All you need is love, all you need is love.
All you need is love, love, love is all you need.

–John Lennon / Paul McCartney (1967)

Love is never enough. Especially when you lack clarity on how love looks or feels. Yet we did the best we could. And our best appeared outwardly impressive. We are fortunate our child selves decided to take care of each other. We are glad we made it.

～

Dorothy sighed loudly. "It isn't entirely a love story, but it still is. You wanted the very best for each other and to be protected, right? The Tin Man said, 'Then I made up my mind that instead of living alone I would marry, so that I might not become lonely.' You and Scott had a better plan than the Tin Man. You wanted to take care of each other. That sounds more like love than not being lonely."

Her conviction made me smile. "Yes, Dorothy, 'love' can be a confusing word. Therapists like to call it 'unconditional positive regard.' I am not exactly sure how to say, 'I unconditionally positively regard you'; but that really is a good definition."

Dorothy laughed. "Yes, though that wording does sound pretty awkward."

We both laughed. But I understood that therapists, more than any others, know how problematic the concept of love can be for survivors who had trusted their abusers' expressions of affection.

5
AND THEN CAME CHILDREN

'I always like to help anyone in trouble,' [said the stork]. 'But I must go now, for my babies are waiting in the nest for me. I hope you will find the Emerald City and that Oz will help you.'

–Oz

With a twinkle in her eyes, Janyne said, "We were so surprised to be pregnant. Did we think babies really did arrive by stork?"

The other two (not nearly so amused) explained to Dorothy that having a baby on the way just short of our one-year-anniversary came as a great surprise.

Jane felt the need to explain further. "My subconscious need to avoid all body sensations now created a disconnect. Symptoms of pregnancy just didn't register. Instead, I thought it was a return of mono exhaustion."

"Yes," Non Janyne continued. "And my solution? Drink cup after cup of coffee, then spend eight months wondering if the caffeine has damaged the baby. Not the best plan."

"Well, we certainly didn't plan for the baby, but no child ever was more wanted!" Janyne exclaimed.

Jane sighed. "Without consciously acknowledging the thought, I had incorrectly believed a punishing God would never allow me to have children. It just didn't seem possible. Pregnancy certainly came as a great surprise! We were afraid and excited. And it changed our view of God."

"So it wasn't a stork?" Dorothy asked with a quizzical grin. "I didn't think so…. How long *did* it take you to figure out a baby was coming?"

"A long time!" the group replied in unison.

Non Janyne began typing.

WHAT'S THAT ON MY FOREHEAD?

Why was I so clueless regarding pregnancy? There's no real explanation. One afternoon while teaching kindergarten, nap time found me in an exhausted daze. I decided to "rest" on the big pillow in the book corner.... Then later I awoke with a start when a father arrived to pick up his child. Wiping the drool off my face and trying to regain composure, I filled the air with profuse apologies.

Sometime later, after announcing my pregnancy, that same father came to me and asked, "You know when you fell asleep during nap time?"

How could I forget?

"I knew you were pregnant then. There's just no tired like a pregnant woman."

Every woman who remembers the pathological exhaustion during pregnancy says "Amen"! I appreciated his compassionate understanding.

Soon after this sleeping and drooling episode, while sitting out in the sun to put some color into my pale skin before being a bridesmaid in a wedding, the exhaustion overcame me again. Heading for the house, knowing how easily my fair skin might burn, I barely got inside the sliding glass door before curling up on the floor and succumbing once again to the exhaustion. Scott arrived home from work and found me "passed out" on the floor.

"Janyne! Are you OK?"

Poor guy. What a scare. But this level of exhaustion baffled me.

On our first anniversary we went to Disneyland and rode all the rides that had "Do Not Ride If Pregnant" signs. Then, during the Electrical Parade, right in the middle of the crowd I had to acquiesce to weariness and sit on the ground. Pregnancy still didn't occur to me as the cause. Then one day I happened to mention to a friend's mother about a weird brown spot on my forehead.

"Let me see that," she said. After a short inspection of the spot, she proclaimed, "Janyne! You're pregnant!"

Suddenly it all made sense. And best of all, what I had thought was impossible was possible. Surely God did love me!

My uncharacteristically full-bosomed look at the wedding had required alterations of my pre-ordered dress. I crammed myself into the "We've adjusted it as large as we can" dress (which never did fit again). If the awareness of pregnancy had continued to evade me, how would I have explained the tight bodice?

As Christmas approached, being pregnant felt no less a miracle than the birth of Jesus. Becoming a mother terrified me but also made me determined to be the mother this child needed—the mother I didn't have.

Oh yes, this child was a gift. And absolutely wanted!

ON THE WAY TO DELIVERY DAY

There are women who enjoy pregnancy. That is not my story.

Learning to control my urges to vomit as a child now meant I couldn't allow it to happen when pregnant. As much as other pregnant women hate to vomit, for me it would have been a blessed relief!—because almost everything made me nauseous.

Both pregnancy and trauma increase sensory sensitivity. When describing my almost violent nauseous reactions during pregnancy, many respond with mutual experiences. But my reactions seemed so extreme. Maybe it had to do with subconsciously not allowing myself to feel body sensations. Now, the discomfort of pregnancy was too much to ignore, and it was overwhelming. A slight breeze on my face sent me into a panic attack—even when caused by the simple act of fanning through the pages of a book.

In addition to this misery, I battled uncontrollable weight gain.[14] ACE (Adverse Childhood Experiences) research connects obesity and childhood trauma, and there is some evidence that excessive, inexplicable weight gain during pregnancy may also be connected to high ACE scores.[15] Since childhood trauma wasn't on anyone's radar at the time, the problem seemed to be the out-of-control cravings of a pregnant woman in denial.

Scott accompanied me to doctor appointments to defend me. "She doesn't overeat," he tried to explain.

Maybe they thought, "She sneaks food behind his back, then." Evidently my body was preparing for some horrible apocalypse and needed to build up a food supply—for two of us.

The number on the bathroom scale continued to climb despite walking every day and teaching a classroom full of active kindergartners. Scott and I began sharing a house with my parents, and my mother enforced healthy eating. The sixty-pound weight gain made no sense! The doctor tested me for gestational diabetes, but the results came back negative. Every appointment added more shame to my lifelong struggle

---

14. An excellent overview of the connections between trauma and obesity can be found at the Malladi Bariatrics and Advanced Surgery website: https://www.drmalladi.com/trauma-obesity-link/

15. Ranchod, Yamini K et al., "Maternal Childhood Adversity, Prepregnancy Obesity, and Gestational Weight Gain." *American Journal of Preventive Medicine* vol. 50,4 (2016). Retrieved from https://www.ncbi.nlm.nih.gov/pmc/articles/PMC4801674/

with weight (which vacillated from near anorexia to obesity).

Maybe the second pregnancy would be different, I thought. But no such luck. Even with being sick all nine months, working full time, and attempting to make better food choices, the scale still tipped forty-five pounds. It made no sense either time, but the ACEs (Adverse Childhood Experiences) research may be my vindication. It was not my fault!

Both babies arrived a week late after several false runs. One night, while anxiously awaiting the first child, on one of my frequent and awkward trips to the bathroom I knocked a water glass off the night stand and it shattered into pieces.

"Scott! My water broke!"

Wild, sleepy delirium rose from the other side of the bed and grabbed the overnight bag.

"No!" I cried out. "Not my water, the *water glass*! Don't step on the glass!"

The sleepy, delirious one fell back asleep.

And still we waited. We repacked the bag daily in anticipation of our first child's arrival. Without the now-common ultrasound technology, everyone said I was carrying the baby high, and so the baby would be a boy. (Is this still a thing?) I'm not sure why we believed it, but we took a boy's outfit to the hospital.

WHEN TRAUMA HAS A BABY

The day finally came when labor began in earnest. My contractions had no peaks or valleys—only relentless pain. My generation's determination to deliver "naturally" made me hold out until the very end without any help.

During the last trimester, I had experienced extreme pain as the baby put pressure on what the doctor explained was my sciatica (though the symptoms didn't totally fit). Now, the contractions aggravated the problem and trying to lay my left leg flat on the bed resulted in excruciating pain.

I now have my suspicions a psoas muscle was involved.[16] Trauma, especially sexual abuse, tightens the psoas muscles designed to put the body into flight mode. Much later, when my massage therapist began working with this muscle, the memory of the pain returned. Our son, born five years later in Missouri, didn't drop until labor began. This felt miserable but likely saved me from experiencing the intense pain again.

Breathing classes hadn't prepared me for the intensity of the pain during my first labor experience. The nurses said it could be several more hours. Finally, in desperation I begged for something to take the edge of the unbearable pain—not from the contractions but from the pain no one could explain. They didn't understand my body wasn't just giving birth, the birthing process triggered a trauma response. I felt frantic. The nurses looked at the chart of my contractions and shook their heads.

Finally, the doctor decided to break my water. Then things got moving much faster! The nurses became highly motivated and exclaimed, "This baby is coming! Call the doctor!"

Later, the doctor said he hadn't expected to deliver the baby so soon. He left to do some work in his garden—and returned in his gardening shoes. I could hear him running down the hall as they pushed the gurney to the delivery room—yes, with my leg in the air.

So awkward.

---

16. Christiane Northrup, M.D. provides an excellent overview of the role the psoas muscle plays, complications from psoas muscle imbalance, and ways to return balance at her website. See "Why Your Psoas Muscle is the Most Vital Muscle in Your Body" at https://www.drnorthrup.com/psoas-muscle-vital-muscle-body/

No one understood what those unrelenting contractions and the excruciating pain were doing to me—and to the baby.

"Stop pushing!" the doctor commanded. "The shoulders are caught."

A monitor began beeping—indicating fetal distress. The facial expression of my good-humored doctor turned serious and intense.

My precious baby entered the world. But as I listened for a newborn cry, my temporary relief turned to panic.

This is my final punishment, I thought.

Then the doctor exclaimed, "It's a girl!"

And they whisked her away.

Still no crying baby. Some terrified part of me kept yelling, "It's my Melinda! Is she OK?"

The nurses hovered over her and a suction sound filled the room. Finally, she wailed. It wasn't strong, but she cried. They showed her to me on the way to the incubator where she stayed for the next six hours.

Once in recovery, I looked through a window and saw blue sky filled with fluffy white clouds floating on the breeze. What a beautiful day. Even now, a blue sky filled with white fluffy clouds reminds me of God's love.

The memory of the excruciating pain faded. My baby girl had lived! Her Apgar score was low but steadily improving.

An exhausted Scott headed home for a nap.

After a few hours, the nurses asked if I wanted to have the baby brought to the room. I needed Scott!—but by that time he had gone to the store for a girl outfit. The thought of trying, without his help, to be the mother she needed, overwhelmed me.

Finally, after six hours, we were all together. As I held my baby girl, the stress of the delivery showed in her remarkable cone head. The nurses said it would round out. But it didn't matter, she was beautiful—and mine.

~

Non Janyne paused. "Do you think this is better understood now? Do obstetricians (or any medical professionals, for that matter) inquire about the adverse experience history of their patients?"

"They should," Jane said. "At least they are becoming *more* aware. When we recently shared our story during two doctor appointments, they listened, acknowledged the effects, and expressed their familiarity with ACEs[17]."

"And they wanted to order our books!" said Janyne—always the marketer.

Non Janyne added, "Yes, the situation is improving now, but that wasn't true in the 1980s. It seemed intuitively true that traumatic experiences would affect health, but the research connecting the two was years away from acceptance by medical professionals."

BIRTH TRAUMA AND ATTACHMENT

In hindsight, with my present understanding of the importance of attachment and the effects of birth trauma, there are several parts of this delivery story that undoubtedly affected my relationship with this beloved baby daughter.

First, she experienced trauma at birth. We now understand that the critical moments before, during, and after birth are crucial to the wellbeing of the child. Birth trauma

---

17. See Addendum 3, ACEs Research, for information on the effects of my personal adverse childhood experiences. While the use of the word "trauma" in this book usually indicates physical or verbal abuse, my mother's mental health issues (also an ACE criteria) played a significant role.

affects babies in many ways—emotionally and physically. Fortunately, in this case the effects were not severe.

After her birth, they did suction her nose and lungs, but maybe not enough. The nurses didn't seem to notice she couldn't breathe through her nose. She struggled to nurse, and this added to my insecurity as a mother. Nursing never seemed to satisfy her hunger, so we had to supplement with a bottle, which she came to prefer. (But knowing the benefits of breast-feeding, I kept at it for thirteen months.) Her first night home consisted of one long crying session. We finally called for help and were asked: "Did you suction her nose?"

"Uh, no. How do we do that?"

Isn't it a wonder that human infants survive at all?

Oh! The bulb thing they sent home with us! When we figured it out and cleared her nose, she released a huge sigh of relief and fell asleep. So did we.

Second, they did not place her on my chest directly after delivery. When this is done, a chemical bonding takes place between baby and mother. Like all babies, she came into the world searching for the mother with whom she had already bonded in utero. (This is a significant factor to consider for those adopted infants removed from biological mothers directly after birth.) She needed me to hold her. Hospitals now understand this!

Finally, she remained in the incubator for six hours before they brought her to me. We missed another important window for bonding. Did it affect our relationship? It is hard to know. But my child development background and determination to be the mother she needed helped me become a very intentional mother.

It is important to know how to repair the trauma and attachment wounds inherent in difficult births. Situations like these happen daily and the medical community is increasingly aware and working to lessen the effects.[18] We can't guarantee every child has a smooth entry into life. But with informed intentionality, we can mitigate the damage caused by difficult births as we care for both the infant and mother in the wake of trauma.

My relief in knowing my baby was alive so overwhelmed me that I never considered how the difficulties of the labor and birth might have affected both of us. Society has erroneously believed that children are resilient and what happens when they are small won't be remembered. But their *bodies* remember. The memory is simply pre-verbal. Bodies *and* minds can heal if our care for babies and children is intentional and informed.[19]

⌒

Dorothy seemed lost in her thoughts as Non Janyne concluded her typing. She had listened intently while Non Janyne typed the stories of the cliff, meeting Scott, the wedding, and the birth of a baby. She asked Non Janyne whether so many changes in four short years had felt similar to a cyclone.

"Dorothy, while healing, I watched the movie version of your story. In the beginning, everything looked gray. Life felt

---

18. The effects of relational poverty during the perinatal period (before and after birth) are "more strongly associated with compromised current functioning than such experiences occurring during other periods. Perinatal relational poverty is a stronger predictor than perinatal adversity." See: Erin P. Hambrick, Thomas W. Brawner, Bruce D. Perry, Kristie Brandt, Christine Hofmeister, Jen O. Collins, "Beyond the ACE Score: Examining Relationships Between Timing of Developmental Adversity, Relational Health and Developmental Outcomes in Children," (Archives of Psychiatric Nursing, Volume 33, Issue 3, 2019) retrieved from: https://www.sciencedirect.com/science/article/abs/pii/S0883941718302851?dgcid=author

19. See: Van der Kolk, B. A. *The Body Keeps the Score: Brain, Mind, and Body in the Healing of Trauma* (New York: Penquin Books, 2014).

that way for me also. And then the cyclone came and spun your house around. When triggered, I would feel this way, also. But I didn't realize everyone didn't feel this way. To me, a spinning cyclone was normal."

Dorothy seemed to understand. Afterall, she had fallen asleep while the cyclone carried her house to a distant land. Then she had felt comfortable talking to a scarecrow, a lion, and a man made of tin. Not much surprised her.

"When we moved to Missouri soon after the birth of our daughter, it felt like landing in some strange place like Oz."

"How did the people in Missouri respond to you? The people in Oz called me a Sorceress at first, but I was 'only an ordinary little girl who had come by the chance of a cyclone into a strange land.'"

"That's right!" I laughed. "When a California girl lands in Missouri, it takes some time to adjust; but much as you grew to love Oz, Missouri grew on me."

"Yes, I did come to love Oz," Dorothy said with a sigh. Then she pulled herself from the memory of Oz and declared, "You should tell the story of Missouri now."

With that, Dorothy and all her new companions joined hands and skipped together down the Yellow Brick Road toward Missouri.

PART II
MISSOURI

Dorothy told the Witch all her story: how the cyclone had brought her to the Land of Oz, how she had found her companions, and of the wonderful adventures they had met with.

–Oz

Dorothy and her three new companions stood on a rise overlooking the city of Springfield, Missouri. They gazed at the green fields and trees stretching toward the city, which almost shimmered under the humid skies.

"I'm glad I haven't arrived via cyclone!" Dorothy mused as she gazed with delight at the green landscape. "It almost reminds me—though not quite—of the Land of Oz." She turned to her companions. "When you first arrived, you didn't know this would be your home for the next twenty years, did you?"

Non Janyne answered with a faraway look in her eyes. "No. We moved to Missouri so Scott could begin college in the fall. We planned to return to California after he graduated in four years. On that first, miserably-hot day, the possibility of staying twenty years would have sounded like a terrible idea."

"But thankfully we *didn't* know what the next twenty years would hold," Janyne said. "The baby and I adjusted to hot, sticky bonding times in a third-floor apartment. Life settled into busy days taking care of a growing daughter, and evening gatherings with neighbors whose husbands also worked night shifts. One of the women recognized what a toll the humidity was taking on us and offered us one of her air conditioners. We were extremely grateful! Our life there soon filled with family, friends, church, and teaching. Yes, the teaching was a surprise; we will get to that. Looking back, the years blend together, though the houses changed and another child joined our family."

"We had a good life," all three said together.

Non Janyne began typing; but then she stopped and her fingers hovered above the keyboard. "This is hard. Life was great, but underneath our happy exterior was a different, miserable life. It feels like two entirely different stories."

She was right.

⁓

The effects of trauma were virtually undetectable during the first ten years in Missouri, but the struggles (physical, mental, and emotional) became intense as I approached my mid forties. This is a typical pattern for most high-functioning survivors of childhood sexual abuse.

The church and college community were crucial to my stability and enabled me to use my dissociative coping skills in functional ways. Eventually the dark and troubling days increased, and I begged God for help while wondering why depression had come, depression in the form of a dark cloud.

The following chapters about the Missouri years are a combination of memories, hindsight, and the writings I did—twenty years later—while processing my therapy sessions. They tell the story of how I managed to live with the coping mechanisms created as an abused and hurting child. My subconscious worked hard to keep the truth from myself so my life could be "normal." This strategy worked, but it often showed signs of unraveling during stressful times. All the warning signs were there; but without an understanding of the effects of trauma—or hope for healing—those signs went unheeded. Despite my remarkable ability to live above it, trauma subconsciously drove my life in ways only hindsight now makes clear.

⁓

Non Janyne was listening. "We have tried writing this part of the book a couple times now, but we kept adding too much information about dissociative disorders—that needs to go in a separate book."

"I see what you mean," Dorothy said. "We can't keep on the path to the Emerald City unless we refuse to get lost in the details along the way."

Non Janyne agreed. "For someone like me, who tends to focus on details, this is far more challenging than I expected."

Dorothy laughed. "You might say we have to chop through the trees to reach our destination."

> *It was a bit of good luck to have their new comrade join the party, for soon after they had begun their journey again they came to a place where the trees and branches grew so thick over the road that the travelers could not pass. But the Tin Woodman set to work with his axe and chopped so well that soon he cleared a passage for the entire party.*
> —Oz

"Yes, like chopping through trees. If I stick to telling the story of the effects of trauma in my life, we can stay on course." Non Janyne seemed satisfied with this conclusion; and with the Yellow Brick Road soon cleared of brush, the small group continued down the path to the first chapter of Part II. They were making progress toward the Emerald City!

6
LIVING AS A NORMAL MOTHER

They looked at Dorothy and her strangely assorted company
with wondering eyes, and the children all ran away and
hid behind their mothers when they saw the Lion...

–Oz

"We do a lot of talking about mothers in our books." Non Janyne was concerned about two consecutive mother chapters. Was she already getting lost in the details again?

Jane sighed. "People will think we had mother issues."

"Well, we did," Janyne said in her best self-deprecating, humorous voice.

Jane considered feeling shamed. But she laughed instead, at the absurdity of even caring at this point.

Non Janyne stepped in. "The previous chapter told about *becoming* a mother; this one is about how the three of us worked together to *be* a mother."

"Yes," Janyne said. "It has a different nuance. But, can we please recount those years without saying much about our children? I may have used them as illustrations too often in the past."

(True. And unfortunately, my students occasionally told my children what I had said about them.)

Jane understood the concern. "We'll be careful, but we can't really be a mother without children."

Janyne rolled her eyes. "Obviously."

Dorothy often found it nearly impossible to keep the three moving forward. She said, "Yes, it does require children. Your son and daughter spent their childhoods in Missouri, so we can't leave them out entirely! Let's get started."

A THREE-PART MOTHER

As the three settled in to begin the chapter, Janyne made a great point. "By all appearances our life was just like those of the other mothers we knew."

This is true. Our life seemed like an endless procession of driving children to church, school, and sports activities; enjoyable summer vacations; schoolwork and projects, programs and birthday parties.

Jane laughed. "Yes, we practically lived in the car. Most conversations took place there."

Non Janyne sighed. "The minivan *looked* like we lived in it: random wrappers, odd pieces of clothing, toys. It drove me mad."

Janyne, not one to miss a witty opportunity, retorted. "Non Janyne, we *were* mad. Just like the Cheshire cat said."

Dorothy giggled. Non Janyne rolled her eyes.

This time Jane moved the conversation on. "We never had much money, but Non Janyne could certainly stretch it."

Prone to pointing out her "stellarness," Non Janyne said, "I'm the world's best bargain hunter! My garage sale finds were spectacular—a talent that came in handy while raising children."

Ignoring Non Janyne's prideful moment, Janyne said, "We did find some adventurous ways to make money. We ran paper routes and had a landscape business. The best idea was going house to house and asking permission to cut hydrangea blossoms, which we sold to a local florist."

"Those activities helped to raise creatively resilient children with strong work ethics," added Jane.

Noticing the different perspectives of the three, Dorothy said, "You didn't know you were living in three parts, right? The way each of us lives our life just feels normal. Look at me. I was surprised when the Scarecrow began talking, but I still answered."

How did I live with these three distinct personalities and somehow seem like one person? I now wonder. But before therapy, I didn't understand that so much of what seemed like "me," wasn't me at all. Living this way wouldn't have mattered if it felt healthy. But on my most honest days, I knew it wasn't. My unhealed trauma caused me to be, among many other things, hypervigilant and obsessive.

～

Janyne snickered. "Non Janyne, you were super obsessive sometimes. This is where the story about the scissors belongs. You did weird mom things."

Non Janyne looked slightly insulted, but agreed to paste in the story.

KEEPING EVERYTHING ORGANIZED

Somewhere in a support group for obsessive organizers, there must be a chair with my (Non Janyne's) name on it. Sometimes the family appreciated this tendency of mine. At other times, not so much. The organizational solutions I came up with were often quite odd.

Obsessive organization grew out of an overwhelming need to locate things in the exact place where I left them. Oddly, this most often focused on finding scissors. The solution? Scissors in Christmas stockings became a tradition—accompanied by a lecture about not touching my scissors.

I accepted the weirdness; it simply took too much energy to locate constantly moving things. Having specific places for everything lessened the strain, but everyone else in my house believed in creative placement.

"No!" I would say (very emphatically). "The scissors always need to be in the same place." This way, it didn't matter what part of me went searching, they all knew where to find it. All three adult selves understood the necessity of this. My family did not.

As a child, dissociative episodes caused me to forget where I placed things (or what I did). The shame created by these incidents became apparent during therapy. The subconscious solution? Hypervigilance and the uncanny ability to spot anything left in an unusual place. Such a great super power! If anyone in the family lost something, they could usually depend on me to know its location.

My mind tracked an astounding number of things—like a camera constantly taking snapshots of my surroundings. Despite this, scissors presented a unique challenge and needed to remain in the place where they belonged. There may be a root cause for this particularly obsessive need that will surface one day. Until then, don't move my scissors!

~

"Yes, weird mom things." Janyne laughed. "But you also knew how to plan and pack for a trip. I needed you to do that, because sometimes I felt the need 'to get out of Dodge!'"

"Janyne loved to go on vacation," Non Janyne began. "We lived in a world full of religious rules—many of which were nonsensical. In some ways, having others make choices for us felt safe. Rules helped me control my behavior. Conforming served as a survival skill."

"But I hated rules!" Janyne exclaimed.

BREAKING FREE ON A ROAD TRIP

These completely differing sides to my personality must have sometimes confused my children. As a rule-breaking conformist, the solution was to take several extended summer trips where Janyne could enjoy her freedom and, upon return, agree again to Non Janyne's control. In preparing for trips, Non Janyne planned the details and packed the car with activities to keep the children occupied. Janyne climbed into the car with great anticipation. As the traveler and explorer, she loved to put on her forbidden slacks and take an out-of-state vacation!

Those trips remain our best family memories. We enjoyed taking unfamiliar routes to explore the world. However, vacations made on a limited budget usually involved visiting family. And that would occasionally present challenges.

While visiting my parents, where junk food was taboo, we would keep our snacks in the car and "go to the park." We did go to the park, but playing there wasn't always the purpose. Janyne relished working around such rules.

We drove to the ocean and ran in the waves; collected seashells and carefully carried them home; learned about the California missions; and followed the Oregon Trail. Everyone enjoyed a road trip with Janyne, the wife and mother who came out on vacations but didn't consistently show up in everyday life.

I regret that I didn't allow this fun-loving mother to show up more often. She tried—always with some sort of mischief. When present, her laughter filled the house. If she had been given the freedom to raise the children, there would have been more adventures, music, practical jokes, and ditching of responsibilities. Life would have been fun, but my children might not have done as well in the chaotic, rule-breaking home she would have created. The other two adult selves did provide balance.

～

With a perplexed frown, Dorothy commented, "So, you were like the Great Wizard who could change himself into different things just like the man in the farmhouse said...."

... 'You see, Oz is a Great Wizard and can take on any form he wishes. So that some say he looks like a bird; and some say he looks like an elephant; and some say he looks like a cat. To others he appears as a beautiful fairy, or a brownie, or in any other form that pleases him. But who the real Oz is, when he is in his own form, no living person can tell.'

—Oz

"I expected to see all those things, but not a giant head," said Dorothy. "Then, to the others he appeared as a lovely lady, a beast, and a ball of fire. It confused us." She gazed at Non Janyne a moment. "Did *your* appearance change at different times?"

"Oh my, I can see why you might think that," Non Janyne said. "We always looked the same, just acted differently."

"Oh good. I'm relieved to hear this. It's weird to think you might start changing how you look."

"True, but looking the same while having different personalities was at times confusing to my children. I didn't understand this until I heard my then-adult daughter say that she wasn't ever sure, as a child, which mother would show up. I can best explain this by sharing a story that happened many years later."

WHICH MOTHER WILL SHOW UP?

After several months of therapy in my early sixties, evidence was mounting that I had lacked emotional presence as a mother. When healing had progressed enough to enable me to accept my story and to be vulnerable about the ways it impacted my role as a mother, I invited my daughter to a therapy session with me. The time had come to put my beliefs about the importance of changing generational patterns into action.

My adult daughter sat on the therapy couch across from me. Dr. Sue and I agreed that this would be a time for me to listen—not defend, correct, or explain my side of things. My own healing helped me to understand my daughter's perceptions were *her* reality; and at the end of the day, they might not exactly fit my interpretation, but they were still valid—and possibly closer to reality than my more comfortable version.

After listening, I explained living as a three-part mother. This felt like one of the bravest of all the brave moments in my life. Like everyone else who knew me well, my daughter recognized these three adult selves. In the same calmness exhibited by her father, she said, "I always wondered which mother was going to show up."

Fair enough.

Though difficult, the session went better than expected. My daughter amazed me. No one wants to sit in a therapist's office and have his or her mother describe mental illness of the magnitude of a dissociative disorder. It's not something anyone places on a mother-daughter bucket list. My emotional stability probably didn't yet warrant this level of bravery, but my determination to end the generational pattern of silence won.

Relational repair, when received on both sides, removes the pain from the past just like it soothes a child with hurt feelings. Honest and vulnerable confession along with self compassion promotes healing backwards. It helps our children recognize and understand generational patterns. And when that happens, we can change the future.

As the session ended, my mind wandered back to the person who raised my daughter. While my mothering skills were far better than my own mother's, my dissociative coping strategies were undoubtedly confusing.

～

"I'm glad we finally talked with our daughter," Jane said sadly. "I tried so hard not to disrupt life. The cloud hovered over me a lot. I would give anything to go back and be fully present for my children. They needed me to listen to them and help them with their emotions, but I found expressing, feeling, or understanding emotions too risky and troubling."

Non Janyne walked over and sat next to Jane. "Motherhood isn't about perfection; it is about being honest and making repairs when needed. It is OK to say, 'I did the best I could, but it wasn't perfect.'"

Jane looked gratefully at this new, more compassionate Non Janyne. "We did our best to be a good mother, but mothering required much more effort from us than it should have. We didn't know it wasn't that hard for everyone else. When we heard women talk about how demanding mothering was, we just assumed our experience was normal like many of theirs. But it really wasn't, was it?"

"No, it wasn't normal," Non Janyne responded. "Parenting with PTSD is fraught with difficulty. PTSD wasn't an official diagnosis until after the Vietnam War (recognized in 1980). It was a diagnosis primarily for the military veterans—not sexually abused women, and certainly not children. In all my struggles, I just assumed I had inherited anxiety and depression from my mother. It was just who I was."

"It's like the Lion!" Dorothy declared. "He said almost the same thing when I called him a coward!"

'I know it,' said the Lion, hanging his head in shame.
'I've always known it. But how can I help it?'
—Oz

"Well, isn't that interesting ... and sad," Non Janyne said. "Maybe we need to talk about all the specific ways PTSD (CPTSD / Developmental Trauma[20]) affected us."

"That makes sense," Dorothy said. "And now it's time we continued down the Yellow Brick Road to the next chapter."

---

20. Complex PTSD (CPTSD) is a better descriptor of the effects of repeated early childhood developmental trauma. The DSM-5 currently does not list either Developmental Trauma or Complex PTSD and I therefore have chosen to only use the diagnosis of PTSD in this book. This is unfortunate because they are different and require different therapy approaches. For a full explanation of the similarities and differences between PTSD and CPTSD, see: "What to Know about Complex PTSD," *Medical News Today Newsletter* (August 28, 2018), https://www.medicalnewstoday.com/articles/322886.php#symptoms

7
LIVING WITH ACEs AND PTSD

'You bear upon your forehead the mark of the Good Witch's kiss, and that will protect you from harm.'
–Oz

Non Janyne looked at the other two adults. "How do we explain how our coping strategies just seemed like 'us'? This involved much more than hypervigilance. For instance, how do we explain the constant fear of doing something we would never choose to do?"

"Maybe we start with parenting," Jane said. "For instance, I always feared hurting one of our children."

"Oh! Hurting the children would be terrible, wouldn't it?" Dorothy said. "You needed Glinda to kiss them on the forehead and leave her mark, so they could not be hurt."

"Yes, Glinda's kiss would have been helpful," Jane replied.

Non Janyne understood Jane's fear. Many who suffer from physical abuse as children do their best to not repeat the abuse with their own children. But, without healing, triggered anger can explode in excessive, rash, or harsh punishments. Sometimes the generational pattern continues as re-enactments of the trauma.

Jane shuddered. "We asked Scott to be ready to come home if we needed him. This happened a couple times when we felt the uncontrollable rage coming over us.... Once in a dream, while trying to spank one of our children, my hand got stuck in the air. I don't remember getting spanked as a child (nor do my brothers), so maybe the dream represented the fear of hurting my own children."

"Maybe so," Non Janyne said. "There is more I could say about this."

Janyne laughed. "You're feeling the need to expound a bit, aren't you?"

Yes, she was; and everyone agreed that sometimes Non Janyne would need to *be* the topic of discussion as well as to write it.

FEAR, ANGER, AND CONTROL

Most of the discipline strategies of the past century (maybe throughout history) have revolved around controlling children's behaviors. Church teachings most often attributed children's "bad" behavior to an inborn sinful nature and/or lack of parental control. Most Christian teachings that recommended forms of discipline leaned heavily on punishment (spanking, isolation, or loss of privilege). Sadly, though, if a child is hiding a secret, punishment only drives it deeper—as it did with me.

Healing would have allowed me to view behavior (both mine and my children's) through a lens of unmet needs vs. rebellious behaviors which needed controlling. Now, with a better understanding of behavior as an expression of need, I regret some of my decisions to employ popular punitive discipline strategies. The cultural pressure to parent in specific ways was strong. Parents who used punitive strategies but followed them with repair and restoration, were on the right path. I hope my memories of having done this are accurate.

As a young mother, my intuition about what children needed often didn't align with prominent Christian voices telling parents how to raise children. One popular book began with an illustration of a father using a belt to make the family dog comply. The book included many excellent insights and even discussed the importance of understanding the child's feelings, but the use of this illustration and emphasis on compliance through physical punishment disturbed me.

There were voices who highlighted relationship over control, but the predominate discipline methods involved behavior modification and spankings as forms of control. In many cases, the purpose of the biblical "rod" (guidance vs. punishment) was misinterpreted and then used to support spanking.[21]

Spanking does appear to change behavior, but in actuality only relational guidance can accomplish this. It is common for adults to defend the punitive methods used during their own childhoods with the statement, "My parent spanked me, and I turned out fine." Most often, however, if questioned further, their stories of painful interactions belie the statement. The true difference lies in the overall parent-child relationship and a clear boundary between punishment and abuse.

When I served on a college faculty, occasionally young adults would sit in my office and tell me of their struggles to live independently after growing up in over-controlling (and sometimes abusive) homes. Some carried deeply buried secrets and, like my college self, were silently crying for help. Most appeared cautious about sharing their childhood experiences—especially in the cases of abuse. Some struggled to accept those times when their parents' punishment crossed the line.

Interpretations of the biblical admonition to honor parents created a chain which neither I nor these students could break. Telling the truth about my mother ranked right up there with

---

21. Danny Zacharias, Assistant Professor of New Testament Studies at Acadia Divinity College, provides a thorough word study and discussion of the "rod" in *Don't Spare the Rod! Recovering the Biblical Perspective on Disciplining Your Children.* http://www.dannyzacharias.net/blog/2015/5/7/dont-spare-the-rod-recovering-the-biblical-perspective-on-disciplining-your-children

any other terrible sin. As a mother, I did not want the church to place this burden on my children. I wanted their respect for me to be because of my treatment of them—not solely because of my role as their mother. Not harming my children sat at the very top of my parenting-priorities list.

~

Jane sighed. "This concern about hurting our children was not the only fear we had as a mother."

"No, it wasn't," Non Janyne and Janyne said together.

All three adults nodded, thinking about another deep fear—that the children might experience sexual abuse.

HYPERVIGILANT CARE

Three incidents brought this other raging fear to the fore.

The first incident occurred when a couple asked to take my daughter for ice cream after evening church, but then they didn't bring her home when expected. The hour and a half between the expected return time of 8:30 and her arrival at 10:00 filled me with indescribable anguish. She was three, and this undoubtedly added to my terror. They were a young, college couple who simply enjoyed my daughter's engaging personality. But I never completely convinced myself later that something terrible hadn't happened (knowing full well it hadn't).

The second incident took place in a small store. My daughter hid under a rack and didn't come when called. All mothers panic when this happens, but my entire world went dark. Though there was no possibility she could have left the store, it didn't matter.

The third incident involved my son. He rode his bike to see if a friend was home, but then took a detour on the way back. His sister spotted his bike near a field, but he didn't surface for another half hour. He remembers coming home to a completely unhinged mother.

This unhinged fear without a conscious source could have caused me to be overly protective. But recalling my own childhood decision to not tell things to my parents because they might curtail my freedom kept me from excessively protecting.

～

"I lived in constant discomfort over the children's independence," admitted Jane.

"I, on the other hand, encouraged them to explore," boasted Janyne.

"This duplicity definitely created an inner struggle," expounded Non Janyne. "But most of the time Janyne won the argument, especially for our son, who was born an explorer much like her."

"Non Janyne," said Jane, "there's more to tell about your hypervigilance. Remember when you told Scott, 'Don't ever throw me a surprise party'?"

Non Janyne shuddered. "Oh, a surprise party would have been terrible. We needed plans. We needed to know what was going to happen; unexpected things were very stressful."

Janyne let out an exasperated groan. "Well, a surprise party sounded fun to me!"

HYPERVIGILANT: AROUSAL AND STARTLING

It is hard to imagine spur of the moment Janyne, fearful and anxious Jane, and all-things-must-be-planned Non Janyne coexisting in my adult mind and body. The result? Living my life with constant spur of the moment decisions which in turn caused deep anxiety. There was nothing Janyne wouldn't volunteer to do. Then Non Janyne had to scramble to create a plan while Jane drowned in catastrophic thinking. As much as I abhorred surprises, my dissociative self Janyne constantly plunged me into them—while to people around me, I appeared fearless and exceptionally capable.

One indicator of Jane's constant state of arousal (a symptom of PTSD) was my startle scream. Anything unexpected resulted in a short, almost emotionless scream. It felt like someone else's scream. My mother screamed the same way, so I considered it hereditary. But, since therapy, the startle scream has vanished.

～

Dorothy could hardly contain herself. "Maybe Aunt Em had experienced trauma!"

Confused, Non Janyne asked, "Why do you think this might be true?"

"Because my laugh startled her!"

Aunt Em had been so startled by the child's laughter that she would scream and press her hand upon her heart whenever Dorothy's merry voice reached her ears.
–Oz

"Very possible," Non Janyne said. "It sounds similar."

"Everyone screams, you know. I screamed when the Cowardly Lion roared. But maybe that's different."

The Lion, although he was certainly afraid … gave so loud and terrible a roar that Dorothy screamed and the Scarecrow fell over backward.
–Oz

"Yes, you had a good reason to scream," Non Janyne said. "But just having someone unexpectedly walk into a room could cause my startle scream. Even the toaster popping up could shake the scream out of me."

"Well, hmm," Dorothy said. "That does sound different!"

EMOTIONAL OUTBURSTS AND AVOIDANCE

My reactions to simple daily problems often perplexed me. One example involved misplacing important personal items. This triggered both fear and shame and resulted in toddler-esque melt downs.

Looking back, I now realize this level of fear and panic is excessive. It emanated from deep inside me and resulted in a frantic spiral. The desperate need to hide it and feel in control only added to the emotional overload. Now understanding the way triggers plunged me into childhood despair, helps me to feel compassion for myself.

For me, emotional survival involved avoiding triggers. A key characteristic of PTSD is avoidance of those things that cause the feelings from traumatic memories to surface. These triggers can be anything—objects, smells, songs, words, etc. For many people, these triggers can be debilitating.

Remarkably, if necessary, my dissociative system could override avoidance. This enabled me to "turn off" my anxiety when it was necessary to shake hands with men. This did not, however, work on mountain roads—so I avoided them. Further, it wasn't possible to avoid the many situations that triggered the fear of "my turn is coming"—but the anxiety these situations triggered steadily increased, with debilitating results (as explained in an upcoming chapter).

Shifting between the three adult selves enabled me to control my anxiety in most social situations. Janyne was an extrovert, Jane an introvert, and Non Janyne was noncommittal. She seldom had feelings about anything—and if she did, they were handed off to Jane.

～

"It's like Non Janyne didn't have a heart." Dorothy interjected. "Oz told the Tin Man he was better off without one."

'How about my heart?' asked the Tin Woodman.
'Why, as for that,' answered Oz, 'I think you are wrong to want a heart. It makes most people unhappy. If you only

knew it, you are in luck not to have a heart.'

—Oz

Non Janyne reflected a moment before saying, "Created without a heart … It is possible. It was important for me to not have feelings. But no one wants to be around anyone without a heart. When needing a heart, I used Jane's."

"Well, sometimes you forgot to do that," Jane interjected.

Non Janyne shrugged in resignation. "Yes, sometimes I forgot. People were surprised when it happened."

HEALING TO CHANGE THE FUTURE

Recently, when I was speaking to a group of university students, one young woman asked if my childhood trauma had affected me as a mother. I wished I had this book completed so I could hand it to her. Considering my story, and the lack of effective modeling from my own mother, my effort to be what D.W. Winicott calls a "good enough mother"[22] was commendable. In my determination to be this kind of mother, I kept my child development textbook and Dr. Spock's book[23] on my night stand for years.

Many of us who have lived through childhood trauma did the best we could; but it doesn't mean we couldn't have done

---

22. A full analysis of the "good enough mother" is available in the second book in the *BRAVE* Series: *Jeannie's BRAVE Childhood: Behavior and Healing through the Lens of Attachment and Trauma* (Cladach, 2019).

23. This is not an endorsement of all things Dr. Spock, but he did help me to trust my "mother instincts" and not repeat abusive generational patterns. He never said not to spank as many believe he did. He states in the 1976 edition of *Baby and Childcare*: "I am not particularly advocating spanking, but I think it is less poisonous than lengthy disapproval, because it clears the air for parent and child."

better with the assistance of the trauma-informed therapies now available. The struggles weren't our fault. Now that I understand this, I am motivated to encourage young women (and men) to seek healing for their childhood trauma before they marry, have children, and pass down the effects of trauma to another generation. Even with our best efforts, raising children while still suffering from the effects of ACEs and PTSD will affect our children.[24]

All who have reached out to me know my suggestion is therapy. If possible, I would walk everyone through the office door. Why wouldn't I, after realizing how much of my suffering was unnecessary? Individuals' reasons to not access therapy involve stigma, finances, time, a sense that it would be too painful, and/or the idea their childhood experiences don't really affect them very much. It is easy to miss, ignore, or discount the effects of traumatic childhood experiences in our day-to-day living. I did this out of ignorance, but then decided to tell my story in hopes others won't make the same mistake. Society and the church need to be as supportive of those seeking therapy for mental health as they are for physical ailments. Yes, it is complicated. But the future depends on stopping the transmission of trauma to the next generation.

~

Dorothy looked a bit sad. "You know, Aunt Em did the best she could, but life was hard for her."

---

24. Search for the phrase "Parenting with ACEs" for resources and support groups. Also see an anthology by survivors: Brandt, J. & Daum, D., *Parenting with PTSD: The Impact of Childhood Abuse on Parenting* (2017).

When Aunt Em came there to live she was a young, pretty wife. The sun and wind had changed her too. They had taken the sparkle from her eyes and left them a sober gray; they had taken the red from her cheeks and lips, and they were gray also. She was thin and gaunt, and never smiled now.

–Oz

Non Janyne agreed. "Yes, your Aunt Em seemed sad, all right—just like Jane, whom Janyne always hid."

Jane sighed, "I hid under Janyne's smile."

Dorothy replied, "You felt you needed to hide just like Oz did."

'Here are the other things I used to deceive you.' [Oz] showed the scarecrow the dress and the mask he had worn when he seemed to be the lovely lady.

–Oz

Dorothy always made surprising connections. This one reminded me of my recurring dream of the blue room with costumes. It made sense to have such a room. I wonder whether the dream might be connected to Oz. Literature from childhood often showed up in my dreams and coping strategies. No wonder children's literature became my favorite course to teach!

8
TEACHING IN DISSOCIATIVE PARTS

'No one knows it but you four—and myself,' replied Oz. 'I have fooled everyone so long that I thought I should never be found out. It was a great mistake my ever letting you into the Throne Room.'

–Oz

As the group continued down the Yellow Brick Road, Jane asked a telling question. "Do you think we were meant to teach? Or did we teach because of all the teachers in our family?"

Non Janyne didn't answer immediately. Instead, she thought about Jane's question: It addressed one of the most difficult parts of healing from early childhood developmental trauma. *When trauma occurs before forming a secure sense of self* (she mused), *it results in a life lived to please others, seeking validation (in our case through academic success), and most importantly, hiding the memories and effects of trauma from oneself and others. Our first dissociative split was used to separate the pain of the abuse from the child who still needed to live her life and please her parents. It was this coping mechanism (splitting) that would eventually result in our becoming a professor in three parts.*

Finally, Non Janyne shook herself from her reflections and answered Jane. "There is some confusion between understanding who we are created to be (self) and choosing an occupation (what we do). We were three different people and taught for three distinct reasons."

"True," Jane replied. "You taught because you loved to research and explain things to people."

"That's right," Non Janyne said. "And you taught to help people reach their potential."

Janyne jumped in. "And for me, it was a way to be creative."

I don't know how these three parts worked so well together, but I managed to teach successfully for over thirty years. Teaching became the most consistent thing in my story. I taught preschool and kindergarten in California, then college in Missouri and Colorado.

"Jumping from teaching kindergarten to college seems like a huge leap! Did that feel as odd to you as suddenly becoming the leader of Oz felt to the Wizard?"

Dorothy asked great questions.

Janyne laughed. "The Wizard had the best adventure ever!"

Jane sighed. "Well, you saw it as an adventure, and Non Janyne liked the challenge; but jumping from kindergarten to college terrified me. Everyone else felt great; I was anxious. But there we were. Non Janyne can tell how it happened. But just like the Wizard, I felt like we were fooling people. Who ever heard of a kindergarten teacher becoming a college professor?"

KINDERGARTEN TO COLLEGE

The opportunity to teach at the college level came to me as a twenty-seven year old California transplant, wife of a college freshman, and mother of a five-month-old bundle of girly charm.

"Why don't you apply to teach a course at the college?" my brother asked me after we moved to Missouri.

Always prepared to deflect ridiculous suggestions, I responded with, "You know my master's degree isn't finished, right?"

This did not faze my brother, so I applied, assuming that would end the matter; but the Academic Dean's office called to set up an appointment—with the Chair of the Elementary Education Department!

Walking into the office I nearly drowned in anxiety. Despite this, after a short meeting, the Chair of the Elementary Education Department offered the opportunity to teach Children's Literature. She and I laughed many times over the next twenty years about my wide-eyed expression. Such a brave day!

To me, the classroom buildings were a labyrinth of interconnected hallways. Even though I took the time to locate the room before the first day, I still got lost. When I finally walked in the door, the students were all waiting in their seats. They stood as a required sign of respect. That was unexpected and even a bit disorienting.

"Oh, please, please. Let's not do that!"

The students, barely younger than I, were kind. Hopefully, my enthusiasm for children's literature made up for my lack of experience. Slowly the anxiety subsided. Teaching began to feel enjoyable.

After a few semesters, the question came: "Would you be interested in teaching full time? It will be necessary to have your Missouri teaching license and complete your master's degree."

Is that all? Oh my!

Only eight of the twenty-five credit hours taken in California transferred. Completing the degree before the next fall required me to take a full graduate load for two semesters and a summer. Our daughter had turned two by this time and my course load only lacked one class to be full time. Scott took a break for a semester. During that intense time we caught a glimpse of my (Non Janyne's) ability to focus on almost impossible goals.

⁓

Jane smiled, finding Non Janyne's propensity to point out her own "stellarness" somewhat endearing. Then Jane said, "Eventually, college teaching felt comfortable, but you kept adding new classes and then went back to school. It exhausted me!"

"True.... Shall I list the classes?... Introduction to Education,

Children's Literature, Art Methods, Math for Teachers, Math Methods, and Tests and Measurements. Oh, and sometimes Geography and Social Studies." Then realizing this didn't include Bible and Children's Ministry classes nor field experiences or the early childhood courses, Non Janyne fell silent. Jane was right.

Janyne (the one who sprinkled content with creativity) smiled at Non Janyne's discomfort and added, "I always included children's books. Did you know that there isn't much that can't be illustrated by a children's book?"

Case in point.

TEACHING WITH DISSOCIATIVE SHIFTS

Looking back, I can now see the ways my three adult selves helped me manage the effects of trauma while teaching. Being an effective teacher was only possible because of an exhausting process of patching pieces into a coherent whole. Most of the time no one noticed, not even me.

The shifting usually occurred between Janyne and Non Janyne, but when students required compassion, Jane stepped in. Only when something triggered Jane in some way, did the shifting become disorienting.

Jane sighed. 'You're thinking about the time I cried while handing out tests. The student prayed for Daddy, who was in the hospital. It made sense for me to be sad, but the fear of him dying felt like abandonment. Yes, my sobs were uncontrollable."

Janyne giggled. "Sorry, it isn't really funny; but who could concentrate on taking an exam while the professor was weeping uncontrollably?"

Non Janyne rolled her eyes. "I left and sent a staff member back to monitor the test."

My former students could tell many stories about me—and not all because of dissociation. I occasionally wore clothes inside out (not intentionally); sometimes showed up with mismatched earrings or shoes; and one day, while writing on the board, I heard a snicker behind me, only to find out a price tag on my new blouse still hung from my armpit.

Laughter filled my classrooms. The students needed comic relief, and laughter helped me hide the confusion of an unexpected shift.

During my final years of teaching, I mostly taught classes online. That solved many trauma-related challenges. And communicating through e-mail provided a helpful record of my interactions with students. Before retirement I read over some of those e-mails before clearing them off my computer. I could tell immediately which of my adult selves had written each e-mail. Jane wrote encouraging and empathetic messages; Janyne told funny stories; and Non Janyne, who had high expectations of everyone including herself, wanted students to get their acts together.

TRYING TO ORGANIZE THE THREE CHAIRS

Jane admitted she and Janyne hadn't always made teaching easy for Non Janyne. "We didn't mean to, it just happened. But you couldn't send us away; to be a professor, all three of us were needed. However, we did frustrate you sometimes!"

"That's OK," said Non Janyne. "It confused me when the students impersonated us as an absentminded professor in their Senior skits. They weren't wrong, but it didn't make sense to me at the time."

Janyne giggled.

Still trying to help, Jane said, "Janyne! You know very well that the lower scores the students gave us on teacher evaluations centered around organization! You shouldn't giggle! Non Janyne tried to keep us organized."

"Yes, she did," Janyne said, only slightly apologetic.

Jane smiled. "We understand it better now, since going

through therapy. The person who would leave my faculty office and the one who would arrive in the classroom were two distinct people." ... Go ahead and write about that.

～

"I (Non Janyne) sat in my office and prepared for Children's Lit classes by creating step-by-step lesson plans and placing them in orderly folders with a course calendar taped to the back. The children's books in order of presentation were stacked on top of the folder; and before leaving for the day, the stacks of teaching materials sat on my desk ready to take to class the next morning."

"Arriving in class with the neatly stacked materials, I (now Janyne) began to greet students. Organization is not my thing, connection with students is. But while talking and laughing, somehow the stack became a jumbled mess. The students were fun; it felt like a party. Sometimes we lost track of time and ten minutes passed before Non Janyne managed to take over."

At that point, I shifted.

"And now my (Non Janyne's) neatly stacked materials were in disarray! It never made sense. Everything was in perfect order when leaving my office. Recovery wasn't always possible. Sometimes an important item got buried so deeply in the shuffle it couldn't be found during class—so frustrating and disorienting."

～

"Sorry," Janyne said sheepishly. "But as long as Jane didn't cry, we did OK."

"That is not fair," Jane retorted. "But, yes, it's true. Yet, it was I who made sure the students knew we were listening. Sometimes I cried right along with them."

"Very true," Non Janyne and Janyne said in one voice.

～

"The one perfect teaching day occurred the day the dean came to observe. Since the dean arrived before class began,

Janyne didn't step in to hang out with the students as she so enjoyed doing just before class. That meant I (Non Janyne) could take charge as the 'professional teacher' from the first minute. The dean said, 'It was a flawless lesson.' He likely wondered why students marked me down on organization. I wondered the same thing."

TRIGGERS AND SHAME

The role of professor involved more than classroom or online teaching, though. There were meetings to attend, public presentations and speaking, involvement in student activities, award assemblies, and graduations. These situations tended to be less predictable than teaching classes and often elicited anxiety and panic attacks.

⁓

Jane was suddenly angry. "Remember when we asked to not have to stand at the door and shake hands before the evening meeting?"

Janyne groaned. "They made us sit all day long at the information booth. Boring! We didn't understand why you couldn't just shake hands for fifteen minutes."

Non Janyne now realized how she had forced Jane to do so much. "We didn't always help you, Jane. We didn't understand and we got angry with you. The skits were the worst. Why did faculty have to be in skits? Everyone thought we were all good sports. You felt trapped."

Jane agreed. "No one could have understood. Participating in skits felt like torture!"

⁓

Making a mistake in front of so many people triggered a shame reaction much like a panic attack. Trauma affects step-by-step procedural thinking, and choreographed steps were nearly impossible. I was a perfectionist—but not because I believed perfection to be possible or even necessary. The closer I got to perfect, the less chance of feeling the crushing sensations of shame. Normal embarrassment is different from shame. Embarrassment is stepping in a puddle; shame is stepping off the high dive into the deep end of a pool and not knowing how to swim.

～

A tear slid down Jane's cheek. "I just stood on the stage and stared. The laughter searched for me in the fog; there wasn't anywhere to hide."

Janyne didn't laugh this time.

Trying to find a silver lining, Non Janyne said, "Thankfully speaking didn't present this problem unless it required waiting my turn."

Jane's eyes grew wide. "As my turn approached, the world went dark—like the dark cloud. Anticipating award presentations at graduation filled me with dread from the first day of the school year. I waited for our turn with my script written in huge letters that could be seen through the fog. There was just a little pin hole to see through. When my turn came, my feet didn't seem connected to my body and the stairs terrified me. Reaching the podium and saying three or four sentences felt like a modern-day miracle."

～

Yes, looking back at my life does make it feel like a modern-day miracle. Understanding the three disparate adult selves who walked into the classroom, my ability to teach effectively seems unlikely. Despite the dissociative complications, these three adult selves worked hard to make teaching both possible and enjoyable for forty years. Teaching filled my life with purpose—but yes, it was exhausting. Sadly, I didn't know it could be any other way.

～

Dorothy interrupted. "But all three parts of you were really you, right? You were a funny, kind, and smart teacher. But instead of really being yourself, you kept shifting. It's like the Wizard of Oz. He didn't believe anyone would follow him if he stayed himself. It wasn't true, though."

> *For they saw, standing in just the spot the screen had hidden, a little old man, with a bald head and a wrinkled face, who seemed to be as much surprised as they were.*
> *The Tin Woodman, raising his axe, rushed toward the little man and cried out, 'Who are you?'*
> *'I am Oz, the Great and Terrible,' said the little man, in a trembling voice.*
>
> —Oz

"But once we met Oz, we liked him so much better than when he was hiding."

"That's right. I also couldn't believe anyone would love me if they truly saw me. Dissociation provided a way to not be 'me.' You remained Dorothy even though they called you a sorceress. You didn't have to start pretending to be a sorceress; and the Wizard didn't need to pretend to be someone else. I could have been me, but I learned to hide as a small child; and then I didn't know how to live any other way. No part of me felt completely adequate to any task. The truth is, much like Oz, I felt like an imposter."

Dorothy agreed that the little man had felt like an imposter. Then she said, "But your students loved you, and they probably saw *who you were* better than you did."

"Thank you, Dorothy. I was so afraid of my students learning my true story; but I really had nothing to fear. My former students are now my best supporters. They did always know who I was, even if I didn't, and they have been a great help to me on this Yellow Brick Road."

9
WRITING ABOUT OUR NORMAL LIFE

Won't you tell me a story, while we are resting?
–Oz

Janyne, Non Janyne, Jane, and Dorothy continued together down the Yellow Brick Road until Dorothy, growing weary, sat down against a tree and requested a story.

"Good idea, Dorothy," said Non Janyne. "We're almost halfway to the Emerald City. While we rest here, we'll tell you some stories from Missouri. But the question is, which of us should tell those stories?"

"You know, the Tin Man, Lion, and Scarecrow would have all told about our adventures in Oz very differently from each other," said Dorothy. "Maybe you should take turns and simply tell the readers who is writing each story."

"Great idea, Dorothy! That might help the reader feel more comfortable, since this chapter might feel a bit disconnected—which is how our life often felt. As you have already learned, though, each of us writes in very different styles. In fact, I confess I have mostly written academic research papers—probably not a good fit for this chapter. Janyne's expertise is storytelling, though, while Jane's writing usually includes emotional reflection. Those two types of writing seem like the best choices." She looked at Janyne and Jane questioningly. "But, you two must admit, your writing styles don't mix well. Would you like to take turns?"

They agreed, and immediately started gathering the stories.

JANYNE: Lost Library Cards

Libraries are my happy place and I usually could not be any cheerier than when talking with the friendly librarians at my local Springfield, Missouri library. But on this day, I had a problem. It would be necessary to confess that my library card had vanished.

A very tall austere librarian came to the counter. I had hoped the young, peppy librarian would be working. No such luck. With a sigh, I mumbled the story about how my daughter lost my card (she truly did) and how it needed replacing.

"That will be a dollar," she said.

No problem! I love supporting my library!

As she pulled up my file on the computer, though, her facial expression reflected what she was seeing on the screen. This was not the first card replacement; not even the second and … maybe not the third. She offered no conversation as she handed me a new card. Accepting the card, I mumbled a thank you, and fled.

After an hour of searching and locating a few books, I began to collect myself to check them out. Then my heart sank. Where was my card?

Searching up and down the aisles, on the shelves, and around the corners, I willed the card to appear. No luck. Emptying my purse onto the table and exposing my life to fellow patrons didn't solve the problem either.

It seemed like such a waste to leave the books behind. I had no other choice but to go to the counter and ask whether someone had turned in the card. Hoping the tall, austere librarian had left for dinner, I headed toward the counter. No such luck. She spotted me coming. And she smirked.

Shrinking and slinking toward the counter, I watched as she reached behind her and picked up my card, smirking again.

I mumbled, "Oh, you found it."

The entire situation sent me into a fit of uncomfortable laughter and then, to my chagrin, I noticed the title of the top book in the stack: *Laugh Again*. This created a new fit of laughter while I awkwardly tried to point out the irony of the title. But her stoic enjoyment of my discomfort was not going to end anytime soon. Grabbing my books, and smiling weakly at her final smirk, I dashed out the door.

JANYNE: LEAVING IT ALL BEHIND

It was a blustery winter day and as Sunday school ended, I put on my coat to prepare to go to the next building for the worship service. Stopping at the ladies' room and not wanting to take time to remove my coat and then put it back on, I merely struggled with it, and then dashed off to the sanctuary.

Seeing someone sitting in my pew (third row from the front on the right-hand side) irritated me. But making my way to another spot, I took off my coat and threw it across the back of the pew. We sang for some time and when I sat down ... the seat felt very cold.

Reaching back to investigate my skirt, I found it neatly tucked into my panty hose. Quietly leaning toward Scott, I whispered, "My skirt is tucked into my panty hose."

These awkward moments being so common in my life, he didn't even react as I gave him instructions.

"When I stand up, wrap my coat around me so I can untuck it, OK?"

This he did, with a mild look of delight at my discomfort. I yanked and tugged and checked, then yanked and wiggled and checked, and then checked one more time before returning my coat to the pew.

By this time the congregation was reading in unison:

Brethren, I count not myself to have apprehended: but [this] one thing [I do], forgetting those things which are behind, and reaching forth unto those things which are before, I press toward the mark for the prize of the high calling of God in Christ Jesus.
–Philippians 3:13-14 (KJV)

Composure did not come easily. Lord Byron once said, "Truth is strange—stranger than fiction." I agree.

JANYNE: IN A DITCH

From the bottom of the ditch, the light inside the van illuminated my husband and children. Trying to get my breath, I checked to see if my fingers and toes moved.

Then their heads turned and peered out into the darkness.

"Scott!" I squeaked (like a mouse).

Still not seeing me, he got out of the van and walked toward the ditch.

"What are you doing in the ditch?"

What did he think I was doing in a grassy, slimy ditch?

The edges of the ditch were so slick, it took some effort to extricate my already hurting body. My clothes were disgusting.

We were out delivering papers, one of our great ideas for extra income. Some of the subscribers requested their newspapers be porched and I got out of the van to do that—and decided to leap over the ditch on the way back to the van. Not a good plan.

The next day was Sunday. No muscle had escaped unscathed. My kindergarten son came to my bedside and said, "Mom, you know the rule. If you don't go to church, you can't go out and play this afternoon."

Fair enough.

A few days later a raging UTI descended upon me and I

cried over every pothole on the way to urgent care. After drugging myself for several agonizing days, my doctor at the follow-up appointment, wondered whether I had passed a kidney stone. This helped me feel more justified in every single pain pill I took.

After running tests, the doctor entered the room visibly excited to tell me the image revealed an unusual condition. He had only ever seen it in text books. How special! He showed me the test results and the text book image. They did look the same—to my untrained eye.

He said, "The kidney stones are there in a pocket, but shouldn't have escaped."

So, I had little escape artist kidney stones?

"Would a fall in a ditch and severe impact to the kidney area knock one loose?" I asked.

He stared at me and could only say, "Possibly."

My ditch-jumping days were over.

JANYNE: It's a God Thing

My students inspired me with their humorous antics. They often came to class ready to tell their stories. One day two of them told me a story about their experience while making hospital visits.

As they waited at the elevators, they started a competition. One said, "My elevator will come first."

"No, it won't, mine will."

"You don't understand—mine will, 'cause God loves me more."

"Oh, no. God loves me more!"

They were sounding a lot like Jesus' disciples who argued about who would be first in the kingdom. Just then, both elevator doors opened at exactly the same moment. It looked like synchronized swimming, only with elevators.

My students concluded their story with, "It was a God thing."

Thus began my journey of collecting "God thing" stories.

JANE: God Cares about the Small Things

I needed a dress for a banquet and had spent a long day futilely searching my favorite sale haunts.

When you have no extra money and nowhere to go that requires a new dress, you'll see hundreds of great banquet dresses. But if you desperately need a dress for an upcoming occasion, all the dresses are either too ugly, too small, too big (unlikely), too short, or just too *too*. That seemed to be the case on this day.

Stopping at a red light and resting my head on the steering wheel, I said, "God, you know the dress in my closet that hasn't fit for years? I loved that dress. It was my all-time favorite dress. If you could just find me another dress like it, one I could love just as much, I would be so grateful."

The light turned green and I drove to the last shop, thinking "What a selfish request, like God doesn't have anything better to do than worry about what I wear to a banquet."

As I walked into the consignment shop, a very loud sigh escaped me. Without much hope, I proceeded to the rack. There it was! Not just any dress—a dress exactly like the one at home in my closet. The only slight differences were the size and that it had a collar. But the collar made it even better!

My excitement got me home quickly. I ran into the bedroom, threw the dress over my head, and marveled once again at the perfect fit. Pulling the other dress from the closet, I walked out of the bedroom.

My family stared at me. They knew about the dress I loved which no longer fit. I seemed to be standing in it, but it was also on the hanger in my hand. Not possible! The expressions on their faces made me laugh as I said, "It's another God thing."

JANE: Happy, Happy, Joy, Joy

Our family went out for dinner at a local restaurant and Scott, the kids and I agreed that no one could be grumpy (an unwelcome family trait). About halfway through the meal, I was the guilty one who brought up an unhappy subject. My eight-year-old son immediately piped up, "Remember? Happy, happy! Joy, joy!"

This is kind of how we want our life to be; but it isn't always so. William Shakespeare once said, "When sorrows come, they come not as single spies, but in battalions." And in those times, surely, it is fine to lament.

Life is both sadness and joy.

We had received a wedding gift, a calligraphy piece on the subject of our choice: either Joy, Love or Peace. I chose Joy without reading the entire verse. Then, upon arriving home and reading the verse more thoroughly, I realized the path to joy, not an easy one, required far more than simply *choosing* joy.

> *Sorrow with his pick mines the heart,*
> *but he is a cunning workman.*
> *He deepens the channels whereby*
> *happiness may enter,*
> *and he hollows out new chambers*
> *for JOY to abide in when he is gone.*
> –Mary Cholmondeley

JANE: The Ladybug

(This final story expresses my deep longing for healing from what I only knew as depression. I so wanted to be well; but it would be another twenty years before that became possible. Yet, as I floated in the pool, God used a drowning ladybug to encourage me to be patient until full healing came.)

How poor are they that have not patience.
What wound did ever heal but by degrees?

—William Shakespeare

On a warm summer day I was enjoying the luxury of floating in my parents' pool—on a nifty inflatable chair with a spot for my drink. I was happily alone with a good book. No one was splashing, screeching, or doing cannonballs. There was just glorious solitude.

Then "company" arrived. A ladybug flew right onto the pool beside me. I watched her floundering in the water and was reminded of how life sometimes felt. Inching toward her, I fished her out of the water. She crawled onto one of my fingers and seemed to sigh with relief.

It felt good to rescue a ladybug. She spread her wings as if to fly away, but it seemed she was only trying to dry them. She did this again and again until I wearied of watching her. Working myself to the side of the pool, I tried to put her down, but she seemed to cling to me. Afraid my efforts might crush her, I sighed in resignation and accepted her need for my help. It took some time floating around the pool before she had dried her wings sufficiently to fly away.

Watching her struggle to dry her wings made me consider God's patience. I probably wasn't as patient with others while giving them nice spiritual answers to their problems and expecting them to fly away. Pushing the ladybug off my finger before her wings dried would have returned her to her former plight. She needed me; she needed time.

I was also impatient with myself and wanted to be well— "right now, or at least by tomorrow"—for the depression to end and not ever return! But healing wasn't that simple. It took time.

～

Dorothy, who had enjoyed listening and now felt rested,

said, "You were right, the stories didn't sound like they were written by the same person. They sounded like the Tin Man and the Lion were writing."

I laughingly agreed. "Exactly. And if I had included Non Janyne's pieces, it would have sounded like I inserted class lectures. My brain really did function as three different people."

"You needed a new brain!" Dorothy exclaimed. "Maybe it was so difficult because your brain did the work of three people. You were like the Scarecrow. But he didn't have a brain at all! For both of you, life was much harder than it should be."

With that, she picked up her book, found a page, and began reading:

> As for the Scarecrow, having no brains, he walked straight ahead, and so stepped into the holes and fell at full length on the hard bricks. It never hurt him, however, and Dorothy would pick him up and set him upon his feet again, while he joined her in laughing merrily at his own mishap.
>
> –Oz

"See, you were just like the Scarecrow! You even laughed at your mishaps."

Smiling, I said, "You are so right! I even dreamed about needing a brain—a new brain. But that is for another chapter. First, we should talk about how trauma affected my brain. Let's move on to the next chapter!"

> So, when they were rested, Dorothy picked up her basket and they started along the grassy bank, to the road from which the river had carried them. It was a lovely country, with plenty of flowers and fruit trees and sunshine to cheer them.
>
> –Oz

10
LIVING WITH DEPRESSION AND PAIN

*Once the house had been painted, but the sun blistered the
paint and the rains washed it away, and now the house was
as dull and gray as everything else.*

–Oz

Jane was reading from *The Wizard of Oz* when she looked up
and stated, "Depression felt gray."

"You mean like my house in Kansas?" Dorothy asked.

"Yes, just like that. All worn and dull. The voices around
me identified depression as a spiritual problem, but to me it felt
more like a brain problem."

In my writing from this period, one statement jumps out:
*The best way to combat depression? Think more about God and less
of me!*"

Non Janyne stopped me with, "Sounds like something I
would say. It sounded spiritual, but it made it seem like we
weren't trying."

Janyne sighed. "Exactly! During this time, we sat in church
or chapel services for six hours every week, opened every class
hour with prayer, plus attended women's Bible studies and
retreats. Oh, and then two or three revivals every year. How
could we possibly think more about God?"

Non Janyne rolled her eyes. "Well, we didn't always have
personal devotions. That might have been a problem. But
control seemed like the answer. You know, to 'keep the body
under subjection.' I just kept pushing us because self care
was deemed selfish. I drove us into the ground with religious
fervor."

"So, sometimes you were like my uncle," Dorothy said.

Uncle Henry never laughed. He worked hard from morning till night and did not know what joy was. He was gray also, from his long beard to his rough boots, and he looked stern and solemn and rarely spoke.

–Oz

"Well, I hate to admit it, but yes, this does describe me sometimes during the Missouri years."

"We can't blame ourselves," Jane responded. "We believed our service pleased God. In fact, we thought the more we did for God, the more God would love us. Also, all the busyness helped me avoid my turmoil. And since so much of this involved the church, it really did feel spiritual."

Janyne rolled her eyes. "I wouldn't have worked so hard, but you two—"

True, Janyne would have played more, but she wasn't in charge. For instance, I didn't have a clue why my hands hurt. This piece, that I wrote at the time, tells how God stepped in to help me:

I was a worker. And I loved being at the church. I would help with anything and had my hand in everything. All this helped me feel like God loved me a little more than uninvolved people.

Then one day my thumb started hurting. Silly discomfort. I blamed it on an old injury, wrapped it up and went on. Then not just one thumb hurt; the other thumb hurt too. My knuckles began swelling and before long, my elbows hurt so badly they couldn't rest on a table. Scott helped me cut my sandwiches in half; I opened doors by leaning on them; cafeteria trays became too heavy to carry; and I had to make several trips to my classroom because the stack of books became too heavy to carry all at one time. This made life complicated.

Soon, exhaustion set in and I began to take naps every day. The doctors ran inconclusive tests, but when they said, "Whatever the problem is, it isn't going to kill you," I quit spending money at their offices, and rested—the only thing that helped.

"Our body tried to tell the story," Jane said. "This occurred twenty years after the cliff; but the memories were repressed, so we couldn't connect the dots." She paused to reflect and gather her thoughts, then continued. "It does make sense now. Do you remember how we felt that God came and sat on the edge of the bed? We begged for help. I sensed God telling us healing would come one day."

"Yes," Non Janyne responded. "Our hands got better, but the depression didn't. Not until the day I got stuck in the chair."

IT LOOKED LIKE DEPRESSION

I sat in my favorite green chair in our 100-year-old house. A cool spring breeze, and the sounds of birds chirping merrily, drifted in through the open windows. A piece of paper stared at me from the floor. I willed myself to pick it up, but life felt hopeless.

Then the tears began. I could neither get out of the chair nor stop crying. Why did this uncontrollable crying keep overcoming me?

"What's wrong?" Scott asked.

No words could explain it.

He took me to the doctor.

Our family doctor, who had seen us through many trials since our arrival in Missouri, knew me well. Though he often suggested weight loss and attempted to figure out why my hands hurt, he generally gave me a clean bill of health. My visits were upbeat, so when Scott brought his now sobbing heap of a wife to the office, it probably made little sense. But my inability to explain my turmoil resulted in a logical diagnosis of stress-related depression.

I now know the diagnosis of depression inadequately described my cornucopia of trauma-related symptoms. But trauma wasn't on anyone's radar at that time—not the medical profession, society, education, or the church. The doctor's suggestion to begin taking antidepressants sent me into a new flood of tears. What if people found out? Taking medication for depression felt like spiritual failure. But with no other choice, we filled the prescription.

~

Janyne stepped in to help Jane. "You *didn't* have any other choice. And the medication helped us all. We're sorry we blamed you, Jane. You are the one who held all the pain. We understand now. We lived because the medication helped you not to cry."

"Yes," Jane said. "I couldn't be a mother while sitting in the chair crying."

Non Janyne agreed but said, "It wasn't your fault. I thought none of it made sense, so I did begin researching depression."

"Of course you researched." Janyne giggled. "Go ahead, share what you found out. And be sure to include what we later learned in therapy."

WHAT MEDICATION ACCOMPLISHED

What science understood then about the brain hardly compares to what is now understood. Many believed the cause of depression to be a chemical imbalance in the brain. This idea, widely accepted at the time, explained more about the symptoms than the cause. As a chemical imbalance, the only solution seemed to be medication. This solved the problem but offered no hope for healing.[25]

While searching for information among the sources available during the 1990s, I had two questions. The first: Did medication solve the root problem? No. In this case, the root problem was trauma, but none of the information even mentioned childhood trauma (the ACE research began in the late 1990s).

Medication can never heal trauma. Yet, until and unless healing can occur, medication certainly allows a person to live. There's no reason to shame others for making a choice to take medication that may very well be the key to helping them live—or saving their lives.

The second question concerned side effects. The most common was weight gain. I decided to wean myself from the medication after moving to Colorado because of morbid obesity. My health had deteriorated, and my instructions to my family included, "If there's an apocalypse, leave me behind and save yourselves."

The numbing of emotions/feelings is a side effect I didn't understand until beginning therapy. Well, *numbing is the point*, right? Yes, this works well for those feelings we are trying to avoid, but it also numbs the feelings we want to experience—joy, for instance. It numbs everything. You can't block the hot water from coming through a single faucet without blocking the cold water also.

---

25. Rathje, S., "Don't Say that Depression Is Caused by a Chemical Imbalance," *Psychology Today* (August 9, 2018). Retrieved from https://www.psychologytoday.com/us/blog/words-matter/201808/dont-say-depression-is-caused-chemical-imbalance

Since medication had helped before, I asked about it as an option during therapy. Healing from trauma is an intense process! But the realization that the medication would numb the very feelings I needed to access and heal, convinced me the choice to medicate would only prolong (or prevent) the healing process. If I had been working or raising a family during therapy, my choice might have been different, but retirement by that time enabled me to focus on nothing but healing. What a rare blessing!

But, back in Missouri, the only answer was medication. It's disheartening that stigma caused me to feel so guilty about this. No one would question taking medication for illness not related to mental health.

With the assistance of medication, my life moved on in reasonably balanced ways ... most of the time. Balanced yes, but in healthy "normal" ways? Absolutely not.

THE TRAUMA LIVED ON IN MY HANDS

Until recently, few understood trauma as a whole-body experience. Many types of cognitive-based therapies do not fully address this. Accessing trauma-based therapies is essential (EMDR is one example).

Pain often settles into areas connected to the traumatic experience. It made sense to me when my yoga instructor said women hold pain in their hips. Many sexual abuse survivors know this well. As I healed, the pain in my hips (which caused me endless nights of turning from side to side) began to dissipate.

In addition, processing the cliff memory helped me to understand how the trauma settled into my hands while I was clinging to the tree root. My life depended on it. The following piece written for an online writing class (completed during therapy) reveals a growing understanding of the pain.

It is in my hands. It is always about my hands. My nail technicians told me to relax. "We do not like to do your nails. You fight us. You make our hands hurt." Trying my best to relax my hands was never enough and I felt the shame of not relaxing.

At times, my hands hurt so badly I couldn't pull my covers up over me. The doctor said, "Do you type?" I answered, "Yes, but not much." Her response was, "Oh, then it must be carpel tunnel." It seemed like a ridiculous conclusion, but wearing the braces on both hands provided relief since no one attempted to shake hands with me.

Then my therapist's hands brought healing through the tapping technique of EMDR. This therapy somehow found the "me" so carefully hidden deep inside. The processing of my repressed memories removed their powerful triggers from my daily existence. My hands were the conduits for healing and they slowly began to relax, but not completely.

Then the memory surfaced of a day when the ground crumbled beneath me and I slid off the edge of a cliff. My mind was held captive by the repressed memory of the day I chose to live but almost died. My hands could not relax, because my life depended on them.

So yes, it is in my hands. My hands hold my story. In odd moments, they try to type without computer keys beneath them. My hands are trying to tell my story. Now they turn upward; no longer clinging as they hold my healed soul; and stories begin to radiate outward in glorious swirling word clouds.

While gazing in awe at the beauty of healed stories, my hands that held the pain for so long slowly turn and begin to type. My story is in my hands. My healing is in my hands. Yes, my purpose and calling is in my hands.

BODY, MIND, AND STORY

Healing is a multi-layered process. Our bodies don't always get the message that the trauma is over. Though much improved, my hands still held trauma. I instantly ignored the suggestion of massage therapy, but then a friend connected me with someone who had expressed interest in reading *BRAVE*. We met for coffee and as we talked, it began to sink in—she was a massage therapist. In fact, a trauma-informed massage therapist. It took me a few days to make an appointment, but the experience provided a whole new avenue for releasing what appeared to be an endless well of trauma in my body.

The massage went as expected until she began to work with my arms and hands. The release from my hands felt like energy flowing from my fingertips. I admit skepticism before the massage, but the release of tension from my arms and hands felt both physical and emotional.[26]

Owning and healing our stories is crucial. The ACE (Adverse Childhood Experiences) research is irrefutable as to the long-term effects of trauma. As told earlier, I made the rounds of doctors, wore braces on my hands, and went to bed and slept for days to combat the exhaustion caused by physical and emotional pain. If life became too stressful, swollen knuckles warned me to reduce the stress before my hands became consumed by pain again.

It is important to consider the pain in our bodies as a cry for

---

26. Cutler, N., "Learn How to Unlock Tissue Memory," Institute for Integrative Healthcare Studies (2019). Retrieved from https://www.integrativehealthcare.org/mt/unlocking-tissue-memory/

help. We should listen before we go down a path from which there's no return. My pain forced me to slow down. As a child, the ever-present stomachaches were the only way to escape the pressure of constant expectations. In a sense, the pain provided a form of self care. After the cliff, my hands took on this responsibility. I was neither causing nor responsible for my pain; but without healing the trauma, the pain controlled me in many ways.

Dorothy, who had been listening with a sad expression on her face, now walked over and lifted my hands off the keyboard. As she rubbed them, she said, "Your hands did hold your story, didn't they?"

Thanking her with a smile, I answered, "Yes, they did; they still do."

Dorothy sighed. "We should keep moving. The road is long, but we will eventually reach the Emerald City!"

"Yes, we will, Dorothy. I have seen the future, and it is worth the wait."

> *The road was smooth and well paved now, and the country about was beautiful, so that the travelers rejoiced in leaving the forest far behind, with its many dangers that they met in its gloomy shades.*
>
> –Oz

11
DREAMING ABOUT BRAIN TRANSPLANTS

The old crow comforted me, saying, 'If you only had brains in your head you would be as good a man as any of them, and a better man than some of them. Brains are the only things worth having in this world, no matter whether one is a crow or a man.'

–Oz

Dorothy was looking at a copy of our first book manuscript. "Why did you name it *Waiting for a Brain Transplant*? Were you thinking about Oz and the Scarecrow?"

"Well, kind of," Janyne answered. "But it started with a dream."

"A dream with a big subconscious clue!" Jane added.

Dorothy leaned forward in expectation. "What was the dream?"

Janyne began to read.

WAITING FOR A BRAIN TRANSPLANT[27]
With the typical hustle and bustle of workshop preparations going on about me, swinging doors in the back of the room burst open

---

27. Unless otherwise stated, the text in italics indicates excerpts from my book manuscript, *Waiting for a Brain Transplant*, with only minor editorial changes.

and a gurney propelled into the room. People stared in amazement as the gurney, followed by a line of nurses, technicians and doctors, sped down the aisle toward the platform.

A doctor stepped forward and said, "Janyne, it's time to go, your new brain has arrived."

The day for my brain transplant had finally come! The wait was over!

I climbed on the gurney and waved at everyone as they wheeled me back through the doors.

"Honey, it's time to wake up."

Scott's voice seemed to come from some distant planet. Oh, bitter pill! It was only a dream! Who knows what could have been possible with a new brain. My present one caused me no end of trouble: forgetting things, mixing up words, calling people by the wrong name, misplacing important things (like children), and worst of all, plaguing me with bouts of depression.

As I prepared to leave for work, I considered reasons for such a crazy dream. The previous day, while working in my office, I couldn't keep my thoughts together. This wasn't unusual nor completely my fault. Being a college professor, advisor, jester, and oft times surrogate mother could be distracting. Singing my favorite tune from the Wizard of Oz often helped: "If I only had a brain!"

Then, in my dream, they came to get me for a brain transplant. That seemed a promising idea. Simply trade in my depressed brain for a brand new one. But I didn't discover how this would work exactly, because Scott woke me up.

THE DREAM BECAME A MANUSCRIPT

"That is how a dream inspired me to write a book," Non Janyne said. "But finding the time to write seemed as unlikely as a brain transplant. Our life was busy. Who had the time to create an entire book?

"But it happened!" Janyne exclaimed. "What were the chances? Our friend invited us to spend a week at her cabin deep in the woods of central Missouri. A screened-in porch overlooked a lake—a perfect, peaceful setting for writing. The bullfrog's loud croaking felt oddly comforting. We wrote during the day and relaxed in the evening—such a great adventure!"

Non Janyne smiled at Janyne's enthusiasm. "I spent many months researching and gathering material before that week of writing began."

Jane picked up the story. "You had everything in place, so I settled by the cabin window and watched deer drinking from the edge of the lake."

"It was good you could relax, but an entire book longed to explode from my head," Non Janyne continued. "My small laptop (one of the very earliest Apple laptop computers) felt like an extension of my hands as I began typing."

"How delightful to spend an entire week with a friend and have nothing to do, nothing but write," Janyne chimed in.

Jane loved the quiet isolation, Janyne enjoyed time spent with her friend, but Non Janyne was on a mission to get a book written. By the end of the week, she had accomplished the task. *Waiting for a Brain Transplant* became a trial run for *BRAVE*. I didn't start being brave because of therapy or because I published a book with the title *BRAVE*. No, I have always been brave.

Dorothy's curiosity got the better of her. "Who wanted to publish *Waiting for a Brain Transplant?*"

Janyne looked sheepish. "Likely me—the risk taker. But what was I thinking? What a thing to do with so much stigma surrounding mental illness! It was beyond brave—more like crazy."

"Truly crazy!" Non Janyne proclaimed. "But the manuscript almost made it to publication by a major Christian publisher. It was superbly written."

Janyne giggled. "Stellar?"

Non Janyne rolled her eyes.

Jane sighed, "My coping structures could not have protected me from the negative repercussions which undoubtedly would have come. Fortunately, the publishing committee decided it didn't fit with their current publication goals. I can imagine God whispering, 'No, not now. This will destroy her.'"

"What were we thinking?" the three said in one voice.

TRYING HARDER AS A SOLUTION

In writing the book, I did attempt to find solutions; but without understanding trauma and feeling pressure to only address topics from a spiritual perspective, the answer to depression seemed to be "try harder." In hindsight, this is odd because my subconscious clearly understood that the problem involved my brain. There was a gallant effort to make this point, but not enough knowledge to keep me from caving to pressure.

The brain transplant dream provided a fanciful solution, but when dealing with trauma-related symptoms, it would have worked better than the "try harder" approach which ended up in the book manuscript. "Try harder" approaches prescribe more faith, trust, prayer, and Bible reading—and assume the lack thereof is the core issue. The reason these solutions didn't help me weren't because of a lack of trying. My efforts couldn't lift the deep sense of hopelessness that overtook me on a regular basis.

Non Janyne agreed. "This was all we knew. For many in the church, this is still all they know. It reminds me of a blog post I read, about a hymn writer from the 1700s. He struggled with repeated depressive episodes and survived several suicide attempts. The man suffered for a lifetime in a world in which prayer and Bible reading really were the only hope. The author touted this spiritual path to living with depression without acknowledging mental illness, trauma in his childhood, or our current understanding of therapeutic healing."

Jane sighed in exasperation. "Why do we hold up the unnecessary past sufferings of Christians as the hallmark of Christian living?"

"Agreed," Non Janyne responded. "I wrote about spiritual solutions because we had no understanding of, or hope for, healing. We might as well have been living in the 1700s!"

Jane sighed. "Remember when our friend suggested reading a certain Bible chapter every morning to help the depression? She told us, 'You aren't spending enough time in God's word. I have always found the verses in this chapter help me when discouraged.' It sounded like good advice, but after diligently reading for weeks, the depression only worsened."

Non Janyne looked slightly embarrassed. "I even slept with my Bible, but it didn't help.... I tried everything! Despite repeated failures of the 'try harder' approaches, I still ended the book with an incongruent chapter outlining ways to 'try harder.' It didn't work for me; but spiritual leaders insisted 'try harder' approaches were the answer. So, in writing my manuscript, I included a list of spiritual practices."

Jane, who sat listening, suddenly sighed again (more loudly this time). "I decided the problem must be me—a spiritual problem so deep that all Non Janyne's efforts at 'trying harder' couldn't solve it."

Janyne threw her arms around Jane and said, "How awful that so many terrible things happened to us, and then we ended up believing the effects were because something was wrong with us!"

Non Janyne was a bit concerned that her words in the book manuscript might have made others feel like Jane did. "I hope those who did read drafts of the book, found some hope. We tried to break the stigma for those taking medication for depression. But now we know that survivors often have deep wells of shame surrounding spiritual failures; and their increased efforts at 'trying harder' and subsequent failures only make things worse."

"We only know what we know," said Jane. "As Maya Angelou once said, 'Do the best you can until you know better. Then when you know better, do better.'"

"Yes, and we are doing better," Non Janyne said. "In fact, now that we know better, there are a couple things from *Waiting for a Brain Transplant* that need correcting."

WHAT I GOT WRONG: THE NEED FOR RELATIONSHIP

What I longed for was a relationship with God—a sense of God's love and a feeling of worthiness. Relationship isn't found through trying harder and following prescriptive behaviors. Yet, as humans (and Christians) we fill our bookcases, computers, and minds with "X-Number of Steps to Everything." It's natural to believe our efforts can solve every problem. We can even make our human efforts seem spiritual.

My attempts at "trying harder" were much like my childhood efforts to appease my mother. Our earliest attachment experiences influence all relationships throughout life—with humans and God. The unconditional and nurturing love of a "good enough" mother (or other caregiver) is the basis for sensing God's love. Though my father did his best to nurture me, this building block of relational care by a mother figure was missing, and that hindered my ability to feel God's love.

Experiencing God's love out of an attachment vacuum proved very problematic, but possible. It required a deep relationship with another human who truly knew me, my story, and my pain. Attachment wounds only heal in relationship. Can this happen outside of therapy? Yes, humans have been helping each other heal since the world began. But my attempts to find those relationships failed far too many times. I needed the safety provided by a therapeutic relationship.

While healing, it became possible to separate my attachment needs from the reality of God's love for me. The evidence of God's loving care was before me every day, but my feelings of unworthiness made it difficult for me to recognize or accept that love.

WHAT I GOT WRONG: Spiritually Bypassing Pain

The pages in *Waiting for a Brain Transplant* overflowed with all the spiritual words my middle-aged self could muster. They weren't wrong per se but flowed from a complete lack of understanding about the effects of trauma. The assessment of the problem was incorrect and demonstrates how easily we can fall into the trap of believing the root to every problem is spiritual.

> *How do we change our worldly point of view to God's view? How do we overcome the strain and stress of our daily walk, which often lands us right in the middle of depression instead of on a joyful walk with God? It is a journey to a better way of thinking and living based on replacing self-defeating thought patterns with new transformed thought patterns.*

It sounds so right ... so spiritual.

My approach to transforming the mind acted as a form of spiritual positivity which helped me bypass my painful emotions. These "self-defeating thought patterns" were the subconscious internalized messages embedded by childhood trauma. The only path to healing is processing feelings and emotions, which cannot happen when they are spiritually bypassed. Saying, "Jesus has helped me leave it all in the past," didn't indicate healing, and the pressure to "leave it all in the past" probably increased the likelihood of subconsciously repressing my traumatic memories.

WISDOM FROM THE FUTURE

Therapy helped me accept that my inner turmoil wasn't my fault. It also helped me realize being more "spiritual" wasn't the answer. This was a huge paradigm shift.

A *BRAVE* reader messaged me an explanation of her own paradigm shift:

> You really have no idea how much I was not a person to advocate therapy. It was very eye-opening to hear myself say, "It is possible to have healing from your past and joy in your future … and the answer isn't just that Jesus died on the cross for sins." Not discounting that, but I do believe this kind of thinking has resulted in a lot of messed up people who have no idea how to deal with their very painful pasts.

As church leaders, we should be cautious about billing salvation as the complete answer for deep relational trauma. Most will need to access professional trauma-informed therapeutic care but will not do so if they believe it's a spiritual problem.

After Ten's experience, for me the solution probably couldn't ever be found inside the church. I can't imagine anyone trying any harder, but my complete immersion in all things spiritual would never heal the little girl inside of me who needed someone to believe her, tell her it wasn't her fault, care deeply, and guide her to healing. Sadly, Ten knew exactly what she needed, but the camp counselor did not.

Repressed trauma had wound itself all through my spiritual journey. For those like myself, who came to faith early in life but were also abused within the context of the church, finding the answer to childhood pain solely through spiritual pursuits is nearly impossible. And, sadly, we believe the problem is us.

When those who claim to represent God, sexually abuse children, the damage is exponential. No one without this experience can fully comprehend the ways this type of abuse destroys the very foundations of faith. If my subconscious had allowed me to consciously remember the abuse or Ten's camp memory, I might very well have walked away from the church. Instead, I stayed, served, and dissociated from my suffering.

Over the years, the many warnings against accessing psychotherapy were hard to ignore: "Going to a therapist will destroy your faith," they said. I believed them at the time I was writing *Waiting for a Brain Transplant*. I talked about mental health in the manuscript, and only mentioned therapy once as an aside in a list of treatment options, but I never suggested it as a viable option for helping depression. The warnings caused me to fear the very thing that could have helped me. My faith journey eventually found healing *because* of professional therapy, not by avoiding it.[28]

~

As I typed the last words, Dorothy leaned forward and began talking so fast, she forgot to breathe.

"All the people made me afraid of Oz. He certainly wasn't God, but he wasn't 'Oz the Terrible,' either. In the end we became friends and tried to solve our problems together."

> *But the people remembered him lovingly, and said to one another: 'Oz was always our friend. When he was here he built for us this beautiful Emerald City and, now he is gone, he has left the Wise Scarecrow to rule over us.' Still, for many days they grieved over the loss of the Wonderful Wizard, and would not be comforted.*
> —Oz

---

28. Note: See https://www.janyne.org/findtherapist for guidelines to access trauma-informed therapy.

"See?" Dorothy continued, "All that stuff about Oz being terrible could have kept me from reaching the Emerald City! And when people made *you* afraid, it kept you from going to therapy for many years. God wanted you to heal and what they said almost kept you from going and experiencing healing!"

"Yes, this was part of my fear on that first day of therapy," Jane said. "Thankfully, though, I walked through the door."

"It is good you did," Dorothy said adamantly. Then she laughed. "Listen to us. We have moved ahead in our story to Colorado again without even finishing Missouri."

Everyone looked a bit sheepish and Non Janyne, with an apologetic look, said, "But we need to talk a bit more about the book manuscript, *Waiting for a Brain Transplant*, because in many ways the writing did help us. Just because we couldn't yet access therapy didn't mean that God wasn't helping us."

"Very true," Jane said. "We did have faith, it just got all wound up with trauma. God understood."

Then taking Dorothy's hand, Jane led the group to the next chapter.

12
LIVING A TRAUMA-BASED FAITH

'Can't you give me brains?' asked the Scarecrow.
'You don't need them. You are learning something every
day. A baby has brains, but it doesn't know much. Experi-
ence is the only thing that brings knowledge, and the longer
you are on earth the more experience you are sure to get.'
–Oz

Dorothy watched the three adults as they began working on this chapter. "You know, the Wizard of Oz believed the Scarecrow would learn all he needed to know through experience. Your experiences weren't great. I can see it might have been a problem."

Non Janyne nodded in agreement. "It certainly was a problem! We had all sorts of incorrect internalized messages that made life challenging and often got tangled with faith."

"With faith?" Dorothy was confused. "How?"

Non Janyne smiled. "It's complicated, but sometimes we turned incorrect beliefs into spiritual 'strengths.' This will be challenging to explain, but the best example is about choices."

Dorothy settled in to listen. She had a feeling this wouldn't stay linear.

It didn't.

THE PROBLEM WITH CHOICES

"OK, that works. Let's talk about choices," Jane said. "I think many survivors struggle with this. It is hard for them to believe they have a choice or are capable of making the right choices. I don't think we're the only ones who have felt that way."

"I don't think so, either," Non Janyne said. "Do you remember how the topic of choices kept showing up in my writing?"

"True," Jane responded. "I recall a very lengthy discussion of choices at the end of *Waiting for a Brain Transplant*. It felt out of place to me."

Janyne agreed. "But it's true, we were always obsessed by choices. In fact, therapy began with trying to choose whether or not to sign the faculty contract for the next year. How confusing to try to make a choice, not be able to make a choice, and believe I didn't really have a choice—all at the same time. It made no sense."

Non Janyne laughed. "Janyne, you're talking in circles again. But no, it didn't make sense ... until we remembered this poem."

THE MEMORIES OF CHOICE

Choices
made in a moment
lived for a lifetime.

Decisions
made by the heart
fought by the mind.
Weak moments
and never-ending memories.

If one could only see
the memories our choices make,
if we could but understand
that the pain of some decisions
will never heal this side of Heaven.

Jane sighed. "I remember writing that at a time when I was paralyzed by fear of making a choice—on top of living with the pain of previous decisions." Then, unexpectedly, she laughed. "How did I sneak the poem into the manuscript, anyway? Did you lose control, Non Janyne?"

Non Janyne blinked. "Possibly." She seemed perplexed. "But what I wrote after the poem portrayed no emotion."

Sometimes, in our effort to emphasize the forgiving nature of God, we tend to neglect the undeniable fact that forgiveness does not erase memories or consequences. What we choose to do lives with us always. We can believe, understand, and fully accept God's forgiveness. We can even forgive ourselves, but the memories can never be erased. This can be depressing unless one deals with it appropriately, by accepting our responsibility and forgiving others and ourselves.

Non Janyne sighed loudly. "Ugh. 'Deal with it appropriately and accept responsibility.' Yes, this was me! And then I followed it with a 'forgiveness prescription.' Sorry. I truly did lack compassion!"

Jane patted Non Janyne on the shoulder and said, "It's OK, we have all grown a lot. But it's clear that we had no hope the pain could ever be gone. No wonder the healing effects of EMDR therapy felt like a miracle. The pain really could be gone."

This reminder of the joy healing had brought caused an impromptu group hug. Even Dorothy joined in.

Then Jane spoke again. "The memory of the cliff now can exist without drowning me in suffocating shame, because I recognized and healed the false internalized message. I did not choose what happened that day before driving to the cliff. No, it wasn't my fault."

Janyne and Non Janyne cheered. This healed Jane was awesome!

A SPIRITUAL FEAR OF CHOICES

Healing traumatic memories, while an important part of therapy, was not where the deepest work around choices took place.

Relational trauma inflicted by those I trusted had caused me to believe the abuse had been my choice.

When I was three years of age, a man I trusted asked, "Jeannie, do you want to go outside and play with the others or stay here inside with me and play with the blocks?" I chose to stay inside and play blocks with the man who became my abuser. No wonder making the simplest of choices filled me with fear!

Dorothy looked sad, and Jane leaned down to talk to her. "Sometimes terrible things happen to small children. We were very small; and eventually we didn't consciously remember what happened. But it was still always difficult to make decisions. Healing helped us understand why choices were so difficult."

"That must have been challenging." Dorothy said. "For me, being afraid of making choices would have made traveling down the Yellow Brick Road impossibly difficult!"

Non Janyne agreed. "Our fear of making choices caused us to want God (and others) to make choices for us. In *Waiting for a Brain Transplant* I wrote, 'Our most important choice is to keep our eyes on God and allow Him to guide us.' It was really more than 'Guide us'; it felt more like 'Tell me what to do.'"

～

Listening to God's guidance is important, but it became an obsession. I wore my "obedience" like a badge of courage while hiding distrust for my own ability to make choices.

My obsessive desire to obey God felt spiritual and my choice-making dysfunction morphed into a spiritual strength. Choices based in absolute obedience were often terrifying— oddly confirming them as correct.

I didn't consider it faith unless it terrified me.

Is faith challenging at times? Absolutely. But without access to feeling safe in the world, there can be no peace that passes understanding. Even good choices drowned me in catastrophic thinking.

During those years, was I following God? Yes. But it never felt like relationship. God wanted a better life for me—one involving inner peace and freedom of choice. Many hold up blind obedience as the gold standard—completely ignoring how biblical characters often struggled with choices before deciding (often even negotiating with God in the process). We erroneously call such a relational process, "lack of faith."

PARALYZING CHOICES

"We wrote a lot about choices in our books," Jane said. "Towards the end of *BRAVE*, I became overwhelmed with the realization that God wanted me to choose whether or not to tell my story."

Janyne interrupted, "While at the marina one day, we were trying to work through this (as told in *BRAVE*). The metaphor involved staying safely in a cove or choosing to adventure out onto the ocean waves. I wanted to go on the waves!" Janyne looked as if she might immediately launch.

Jane smiled at her. "And I longed for safety."

Non Janyne remained quiet for some time before saying, "Our faith walk was based on trauma. So much fear. So many wild leaps of 'faith' based on obsessive obedience to God. We also missed opportunities while waiting for God's perfect will." She paused before continuing, "Then, when we should have made the choice to leave situations that were no longer healthy, leaving seemed impossible, because we believed God had chosen for us to be there."

"Oh my," Jane lamented. "You would say, 'I am here because it is God's will. God will have to hit me over the head with a hammer to convince me to leave.' Sometimes we needed to get out, to take good opportunities, to not stay where we weren't respected. But we didn't believe we could make choices....We wanted God to choose for us."

"To think," Janyne said. "It all began with an innocent choice made by a three-year-old child."

~

In Colorado, my obsession with obeying God created some interesting therapy dialogs. The decision whether or not to sign the teaching contract for the following year filled many sessions with angst. I needed God to tell me to resign; maybe my therapist would decide for me, or maybe my husband.

Someone, please tell me what to do!

Reflecting on the decision to resign, it is clear Non Janyne took charge. Ending a forty-year career on her own terms was extremely important to her, especially after the terrible ending in Missouri (explained in the next chapter).

~

Now Non Janyne sighed. "I wanted my career to end well—to hear God say, 'Well done.' But the darkness … kept getting harder to control. As strong as I was, I couldn't control the surfacing traumatic memories." Then her tone changed. "But retiring felt like weakness," she lamented. "So, I just 'claimed' that God had told me to resign. That sounded spiritual. Who could question it?"

~

It was the best I could do. The truth? I simply couldn't continue working at the college—maybe not anywhere, not ever again.

Most people in my life seemed content with my explanation. But one wise friend said, "When people say they are doing something because God told them to, it ends the discussion." Then he gave me a hug and walked away.

He was right; it worked very well in ending the discussion. No one questioned me.

CHOOSING TO BE BRAVE

My turmoil over resigning foreshadowed my distress about

publishing *BRAVE*. I incorrectly believed obeying God meant telling my story. The belief that I didn't have a choice compounded my fear. I erroneously believed God's overarching plan for my life was to use my suffering to help others. To my mind, any suffering caused by publishing my story would confirm it as being the "will of God."

I didn't think it was about God caring for me, but about God using me—like a pawn on God's chessboard.

Then one day I recalled the time many years earlier when I had sensed God's desire that I be healed. That vivid moment had come long before I ever sat on a therapy couch. God *did* care about me and wanted me to heal! God wanted me to access the abundant life stolen from me as a child! And most importantly, God then wanted me to make my own decisions.

What? *Healing was about* me? *To publish or not publish was* my *choice?* What an absolutely terrifying thought. God wanted me to make my own choices—and believe in them. And again, no one would help.

What if the choice I made turned out to be wrong? What if telling my story didn't make any difference? What if ... what if ... what if ...

Finally, I did choose to let *BRAVE* be published. This choice was based on the ways I wanted to spend the remainder of my life. While important for me to choose, the understanding that God could bring good from any choice I made, freed me from a dysfunctional life of needless spiritual wrestling over choices. *Every choice did not require drowning in confusion and catastrophic thinking!*

Frightening, unhealthy leaps of obedience pale in comparison to knowing my choice is helping others heal. Celebrating *BRAVE*'s travels around the world is better than feeling like a frightened pawn on God's chessboard. I'm thankful for

God's tender leading during my life. And I'm thankful for the patience of a therapist who helped me trust my own ability to make good choices (which, she pointed out, I had been making all along).

If I was already making good choices, why did healing the internalized message matter? Because accessing the depth of God's love requires exercising the gift of free will. Choosing to cooperate with God within the context of relationship feels so much better than blind obedience.

So much better.

⁓

Dorothy seemed poised to move to the next chapter, but then she stopped and looked thoughtful. "I remember, one time, making a choice I instantly regretted."

> *Dorothy was ready to cry with disappointment. 'I have wasted the charm of the Golden Cap to no purpose,' she said, 'for the Winged Monkeys cannot help me.'*
>
> *'It is certainly too bad!' said the tenderhearted Wood-man.*
>
> –Oz

"How nice of the Tin Man to console you," Jane said. "God consoled me often, especially about choices that went wrong. It was especially hard when we thought we were doing the right thing."

Non Janyne agreed. "I ended *Waiting for a Brain Transplant* with a story about how God came and helped me. It is a short story we should insert here as a chapter."

Each one settled in her chosen spot, to listen. This was one of their favorite stories!

13
A BRAIN TRANSPLANT
SUCCESS STORY

Non Janyne looked around at the small group who were waiting in anticipation for her to begin reading the story so familiar to them. She took a deep breath to begin reading—

"Wait," Jane interrupted. "I remember what we wrote in this story back then, and you know we really didn't have any idea why we thought we needed a brain transplant. We knew nothing about the effects of trauma and the possibility that we could heal. All we had was the wish that somehow our brain could be traded for another."

Janyne laughed with surprise. "Both the Scarecrow and I thought brains were the answer to everything, didn't we?"

Jane nodded in amusement. "I don't want to leave the story that way, either. We do need to include it in this book because of how it unknowingly foretold how therapy would one day heal us. We want our readers to be encouraged to know that God often gives us hope for a future we cannot yet see. That's faith, right?"

"Yes, I agree, our writing this story showed our faith in what we could not see, based on what we understood at the time," Non Janyne said.

"But," Jane asked, "what would the story have looked like if we had understood trauma? That is what we want others to understand. What if we revise the story, then, to include our current understanding of trauma but leave the rest of this part of *Waiting for a Brain Transplant* exactly as we originally wrote it. Italicizing what we are changing, will clarify the changes."

Everyone nodded in agreement.

THE STORY

I remember lying on the gurney as it rolled me to the operating room. Upon waking from surgery, I learned the operation took several years.

I expected to feel *Happy, happy! Joy, joy!* But instead, a quieting peace filled every part of me. I no longer felt the need to impress God with endless lists of my accomplishments. Without even trying, I understood how God thought. He didn't care about my continuous efforts at trying to please. Instead, God just wanted the two of us to walk through life together.

As I explored my new mind, God sat down in the chair beside my bed. This surprised me because doctors are usually in such a hurry to get to the next patient.

God asked, "Do you have any questions?"

Yes. But it seemed some of the questions I wanted to ask before the operation had now vanished. Not wanting to lose the moment, though, I began. "Well, I guess I just don't understand why my old brain was so confused."

God smiled lovingly. *"You know, it wasn't your fault. You were born a perfect little girl. I created your brain to receive love and care from a mother; but that couldn't happen, and it affected how your brain developed. I also created you with ways to survive; and when bad things happened, you used every single one of them—but it made your life difficult. It was never your fault and not part of my plan for you. My plan for you was filled with goodness."*

It wasn't my fault.... I let the words sink in and then said, "You prompted me to go to Dr. Sue because she would know how to help me understand this and heal."

God smiled, *"Yes, researchers and therapists are starting to understand how to heal brains and bodies after trauma. I am glad you chose to have the brain transplant. I know it frightened you to make that choice."*

"Oh my! Yes, it did! But it wasn't actually a transplant, was it? The idea of a brain transplant made a great story, and the dream amused me, but what truly happened was healing, wasn't it?"

God laughed. "Yes, I enjoy the ideas your creative mind conjures up. You have been like that since you were small."

God's words settled deeply into my body. They sounded so much better than the painful words my mother spoke to me—words that haunted me for a lifetime. The situations that trapped me didn't happen because of who I was, but because bad things had happened to me as a child.

I looked into God's eyes, and the love in those eyes overwhelmed me. I began to cry—not tears of sorrow, but tears of joy. I had been longing for something that had been available to me from the beginning. I had longed to one day be worthy of God's love; but now I knew God had always seen my worth.

A pen and paper lay on the table in front of me. Picking up the pen, I began writing.

HEAVEN, I'M ALREADY THERE

I've been striving to be what I already am.
I've been searching for love that is already mine.
Begging for gifts already given,
Asking forgiveness for sins not my own.
I've been longing for Heaven,
But I'm already there.

There isn't one thing God has to do.
There isn't a sacrifice yet to be made.
There isn't more Spirit that must be poured out.
I long for deliverance from this world of pain.
I am crying for Heaven,
But I'm already there.

I am hoping I may through effort obtain
The standing of children born to a king.

Somehow live worthy of sitting with Him
And dining in splendor at the bountiful feast.
I am dreaming of Heaven,
But I'm already there.

God seated me there and wrote down my name.
But I'm begging for scraps, not staking my claim.
I am longing for someone to think I am worthy,
I am hoping to be what I already am.
I am searching for Heaven,
But I'm already there.

I am thinking I still stand outside on the street,
Lonely and tired and filled with defeat.
I am thinking that no one, and surely not God
Would bring me inside and give me a seat.
I am aching for Heaven,
But I'm already there.

Now I believe I'm a child of the King.
I can claim all the riches, and power, and strength.
I walk with God, as God walks with me.
I don't have to try, I already am.
I am living in Heaven,
I'm already there.

I finished writing and handed the poem to God who seemed to know the words even before reading them. "This is a treasure," God said. "Thank you."

"Wait," I exclaimed. "There is another question! I was going to ask whose brain I received.... But we answered that, didn't we? I received my own brain—the one I was meant to have!"

God sank back into the chair and gazed at me for a long time, then spoke. *"Yes, it is the brain you were meant to have, but now it is so much more. Your brain is full of the wisdom you have found along the way. It overflows with love and compassion and has learned to write in delightful, thought-provoking ways that help*

143

others understand the emotions inside hurting children and adults.
Yes, it is so much more."

This was true. I had paid a great price for this brain transplant, but the healing had transformed me, and I had no regrets.

God began walking out the door.

I called out, "Do you want me to tell others what you have done for me?"

God turned and smiled. "Start writing."

And I did.

~

"Non Janyne," said Jane, smiling. "I think I might have written that part of the manuscript. How interesting; but writing our story of healing would not be possible for another twenty years, because this vision would require us to go to Colorado and heal. Sadly, more lessons and layers were added before leaving Missouri. I would cry more tears before moving and finally learning the importance and power of making our own choices.

"Jane, sometimes I cried too," Dorothy said. "The Bible says God collects our tears. So our tears are important. Even when our friends don't know how to help us, God is working for our good."

> *[Dorothy's] friends were sorry, but could do nothing to help*
> *her; so Dorothy went to her own room and lay down on the*
> *bed and cried herself to sleep.*
> —Oz

"Dorothy, you do understand," Jane said.

Non Janyne watched the two and thought, "Dorothy understands so much! Her aunt and uncle must have taken her to church."

Then, taking Dorothy's hands in theirs, the small group walked toward the next chapter—this time with a bit of hesitation ... knowing Missouri didn't end well.

14
THE FINAL MISSOURI LESSONS

'This will serve me a lesson,' said [the Tin Man], 'to look where I step. For if I should kill another bug or beetle I should surely cry again, and crying rusts my jaws so that I cannot speak.'

—Oz

J ane sighed. "Lessons! Except for the first section, the lessons in this chapter were so hard. Why did it all happen?"

"Because of *my* over sharing and honesty," said Janyne.

"No," Jane said. "It was *my* pain, anger, and crying."

"Well," Non Janyne added. "No matter how hard I worked, everything still went wrong."

"Exactly. Like the song 'Move' by Mercy Me." (Janyne always knew a song.)

When life won't play along
and right keeps going wrong
and I can't seem to find my way

⁓

My three adults selves were correct in saying everything went wrong; they were incorrect, though, in assuming it was their fault. Survivors are prone to self blame.

Survivors of childhood abuse often unintentionally live as though life is outside of their control, while desperately trying to control it in less than effective ways and believing everything is their fault anyway. Some philosophies believe we bring chaos to ourselves through our thoughts. As a survivor, this feels very wrong to me. Yet my use of childhood coping mechanisms as an adult did often act as a magnet for the hurtful actions of others. The story that brings the Missouri era to an end provides a prime example of this. Was it my fault? No. Was it preventable? Yes. Healing has helped me understand why everything went so wrong and how to prevent it from ever happening again. What a powerful feeling!

~

Non Janyne spoke quietly. "Maybe *you*—or *we*—our healed self—should just tell this. It's a hard chapter for any one of the three of us, because at the time it happened, we simply couldn't understand or navigate it. This was when Non Janyne and I began hating Jane—which was so unfair. *You* can give the chapter the perspective it needs. The readers will still recognize *us*."

I smiled. "Yes, they surely will."

LESSONS AT WORK

This chapter is about work, which in my case meant teaching. Except for taking two short breaks after the birth of each of my children, I worked all the way from college to retirement. They say the average person will spend 90,000 hours at work over a lifetime. My work history surely beats this number.

By the time retirement arrived (in Colorado), the fear of resigning filled me with indescribable dread. One day, just before announcing my retirement, I asked the academic dean, "Will you please not hurt me if I leave?" What an incredibly awkward—and sad—thing to say. The painful lessons described in this chapter brought me to that uncomfortable moment.

This chapter explains how easily survivors become trapped in a web of misunderstood behaviors and choices. I share this uncomfortable story in the hopes that it will help leaders better understand how to work with survivors—even if not recognizing them as such. Trying to control people never ends well, and this is especially true when the people being controlled are survivors of childhood abuse, because in those situations we survivors will subconsciously believe that we are fighting for our very lives.

Please note: The administrators involved in this story were not bad people. They served God in the church, cared for people, loved their families, and provided a positive influence for many. In this work situation, the problems resulted from their power-based, authoritarian leadership style.

LESSON 1: Trust Is More Valuable than Gold

'Very well,' said the Queen, 'we trust you. But what shall we do?'
                                                                      —Oz

Who does a survivor trust? Almost without exception, my abusers were men whom I should have been able to trust. As a result, knowing whom to trust became a complex issue that also caused me to mistrust my own gut instincts. One part of me trusted too easily (Janyne); a second part didn't believe in trusting anyone (Jane); and a third part believed it necessary to trust, but also assumed betrayal at some point (Non Janyne). In addition, my child selves deeply feared abandonment while searching for trustworthy adults. It was a struggle.

For twenty years my department chair, Mary, proved trustworthy. More valuable than gold, she enabled me to fulfill my potential as a teacher despite the effects of my repressed trauma.

Mary knew how to both mentor and "come in low." When I went rogue she needed to address it, but she was able to approach the problem with curiosity. This enabled me to reflect on the choice I had made rather than drown in shame.

A leader who tried to control or overpower me was always making the wrong choice of leadership style. As a survivor, when cornered, I either came out fighting or I collapsed. Neither went well in work situations. Mary was able to work with me without triggering these survival strategies. Her experience as an elementary teacher probably worked to my advantage!

Though my tendencies to go rogue were understandably irritating, Mary remained patient. One year, without her knowledge or authorization, I started a day care and new degree program. Though successful, it did add additional layers to our department responsibilities and teaching loads. The part of me who longed to help the very smallest children simply got carried away with a great idea and didn't ask permission.

We worked together for twenty years before Mary "retired" to begin a new life of teaching in mission work around the world. I admire her gutsy determination to break down barriers to accomplish this.

When Mary retired, I believed I was giving her my complete support, but some of my reactions didn't make sense to her until she read *BRAVE;* and then she realized that her retirement had felt to me like abandonment. This was illuminating for both of us. Outwardly I had shown support. But Mary had also caught glimpses of my small child self who felt emotionally distraught by "abandonment."

It would be a different world if we understood the ways we and others around us often live out painful childhood experiences. Mary both respected and wondered about me; she was one of the few I trusted when beginning to share my story. And like others, she responded with: "Well, that explains many things."

She protected the hurting child inside of me without understanding the source of my struggles. I am thankful for the safe haven she provided for me while I was raising my family. She retired in the spring, and I didn't even make it through another year at that college. The ways she had protected me quickly became evident.

The lesson? Those who are trustworthy will demonstrate unconditional value and regard; they do not try to overpower or control. This became my litmus test for leaders.

LESSON 2: HONESTY IS LESS VALUABLE THAN SILENCE

Just like the Tin Man needing to be careful on the Yellow Brick Road, it became important for me to tread carefully among those who held authority at the college in Missouri. Unfortunately, after twenty peaceful years, I took a wrong step.

It all started with a choice (see the problem?) to teach online for a college of a different denomination. Both were Christian colleges, and this seemed a good avenue for extra income. Many of my colleagues worked second jobs in churches, so as a teacher-educator, my teaching online education courses from a distance, seemed like a good fit. And I thought it logical to inform the administration of the second job. To my surprise, though, I was told to quit teaching for the other college.

Now I was trapped in an impossible situation since I had recently been accepted into a doctoral program and I needed that extra income to pay tuition for the doctoral classes. The online class I was teaching had already started, and I didn't know what else to do but continue. The administrator gave permission to finish teaching the current class but not to continue with that assignment the next semester.

I suspected it might be a doctrinal issue between the two colleges/denominations, and I asked the administrator whether teaching online at a secular college might be acceptable. The answer? Yes, because that wouldn't pose a doctrinal conflict. Then I understood. Nevermind that the online course was a math methods course and involved no doctrinal subject matter, it was being offered through a college of a different denomination with different theological distinctives. I was an educator, and though they may not have understood this, the doctrinal issue never crossed my mind before that conversation.

Then, the other college approached me about a faculty position for the following year. When a friend (who should not even have known about this situation) asked me if it was true, it seemed like a good idea to be up front and honest with everyone involved, including my newly-appointed department chair. I thought this proactive move would prevent further conflict or misunderstanding that might occur if the administration heard about it through the grapevine.

Wrong again. The new department chair shared my explanation with the administration, and they took it as a resignation—at the end of the fall semester.

But it wasn't a resignation. Why would any educator resign midyear?

So, I appealed the decision by writing a document trying to clarify the misunderstanding. In a subsequent meeting with the administration, they questioned me for two hours and insisted my explanation signified an official resignation.

In *Jeannie's BRAVE Childhood*, I tell the story of Five, who could not tell a lie against herself. My grown-up version of Five sat in the room with three administrators for two solid hours and refused to tell a lie against herself. She hadn't resigned and couldn't say she had. This small part of me stood her ground as if her life depended on it.

Since the administration could not pressure me into an admission of resigning, they set to work on a plan to terminate my employment.

The lesson? Honesty and good intentions do not guarantee understanding and care from those in leadership. For the sake of survival, silence is always a better choice.

LESSON 3: Internalized Powerlessness Repeats
When difficult experiences keep repeating in others' lives, it's

easy to say, "There's a reason!" Unfortunately, some of those in my religious world convinced me that God was teaching me a lesson, and until I learned the lesson, it would keep repeating.

Yes, as evidenced by common themes in this book, my problems did keep repeating, but this wasn't because of God's attempts to teach me a lesson. What an unfortunate view of God.

My role as a powerless victim caused me to stay in situations in which all the warning signs were telling me to leave. Just like an abused child, I thought my efforts to be good would keep others from hurting me. As mentioned earlier, this often resulted in excessive openness and honesty. The compulsion to over explain my actions felt overpowering.

For survivors whose main objective is safety, the working world holds many land mines. Their longing for acceptance, dedication to pleasing, and often obsessive work ethic makes them great employees—until trapped in a situation like this one.

When my survival strategies kicked in, those in authority perceived them as something different—like insubordination. Survival wore many faces, and the least effective one was trying to persuade others of my innocence.

Yes, my struggles with those in power over me were a repeating pattern. No, God wasn't trying to use them to teach me a lesson. It is more likely that God whispered in the ears of those trying to control me, saying, "Look past what makes you angry. You don't know her story. If you listen and talk with her without trying to be in control, this can be worked out."

Sometimes they listened and sometimes they didn't. Inside me a little girl didn't feel safe but tried to be good. When she got in trouble, it wasn't intentional. No one could be any more surprised when things went wrong.

Sadly, before I understood and healed my story, I often chose to work for those who needed to feel in control. When triggered, it became impossible for me to navigate without conflict.

My desire to please and try to make things right usually worked against me.

The lesson? My efforts at pleasing and being good are never adequate. I needed to work harder to please and learn to control myself better.

LESSON 4: EMOTIONS HAVE NO VALUE

It's impossible to know what discussion and decision making took place after my two-hour inquisition, but the schedule for the spring semester did not list me as the instructor for my courses. Sitting across from my students at registration and enrolling them for the "instructor to be named" classes was wrenching—especially since no one informed me of any decision on the appeal. I remember that day as a silent scream.

Sometime later a letter arrived in my faculty mailbox stating my employment was terminated as of the end of the semester "for financial reasons." The official announcement: 1) I had accepted a faculty position at another college for the next school year, and 2) I planned to leave midyear (neither of which was true).

The bright spot in all this was my students (who did not know this story). The seniors threw an "all in black" mourning party for me with mementos of our shared experiences. My former students from this college and the next have been my greatest supporters since the publication of BRAVE. They are living lives of service, kindness, and compassion. They are still my "kids!"

Reflecting on those last months in Missouri is still agonizing. My "work ethic" convinced me to take the high road. This meant attending every faculty meeting, chapel, staff meeting, student activity, and function. Finally, in an insurance meeting (for my cancelled insurance), I started crying right in the middle of the closing prayer. A petition for God to care for the welfare of the staff and faculty overcame me in a wrenching, little girl, "ugly crying" explosion. The acoustics in the music performance hall, where the meeting took place, created a spectacular amplification of my sobs. But frozen in place, I couldn't leave.

My complete lack of control was incomprehensible. The sobs were an extraordinary demonstration of everything I hated about the part of me I eventually called "Jane."

Nothing could stop the train wreck. The man offering the prayer just kept praying. There I stood sobbing uncontrollably, until someone finally dismissed the meeting.

This story provides a glimpse of my precarious emotional state as Missouri ended. The stress of those final months probably brought me closer to collapse than at any time in my adult life. My lack of any form of self care during all this astounds me. Going to every function as if it would make a difference in the outcome only added to my stress. My interpretation of "taking the high road" only made things worse.

Holding my head high *did not* require attending a pointless insurance meeting. It felt like a child trying to persuade her mother she was a good girl. Nothing would ever alter what the administration believed about the situation. The outcome wouldn't change no matter how hard I tried.

The lesson? The overwhelming turmoil inside me had the potential to destroy my life. My emotional display ended any tolerance of Jane. Such a shameful public display of weeping must never happen again. Pushing the darkness deeper was the only way to survive.

TAKING BAGGAGE WITH ME

Survivors of childhood abuse are consistently misjudged, mistreated, and fired (in and out of church ministries). The stories others share with me indicate that I am not alone. Even for those without trauma histories, the lack of compassion by leaders is profoundly damaging.

This isn't about poor performance or immoral employees; in fact, it often happens to the best employees. During the two-hour meeting, I asked if there were marks against me in my file. The thick file contained twenty years of records. The dean said, "No, there hasn't ever been a problem or complaint. Your evaluations are all exemplary."

Employees, especially exemplary ones, have reasons for sudden unexplained choices and behaviors. The college lost a valuable employee because they could not look beyond the need for control. It would have turned out much better if they had "come in low" with curious compassion, listened, and tried to find a solution to the impasse.

Control isn't the answer.

This chapter began with the story of Mary, who knew how to "come in low." She did approach situations with curious compassion. It reminds me of the interactions between Jesus and Peter. We need to take this example and apply it in families, churches, communities, and places of employment. We could redeem so many situations with this simple change in our thinking.

On the other side of this issue, is the survivor's need for healing. Without healing, it wasn't possible to stop myself from charging at the bull again and again. My deep well of shame compelled me to constantly seek validation from those most interested in controlling my behaviors. Self care isn't likely to be a priority for those who do not feel worthy. Only healing and finding a sense of worth within myself could have ever stopped this destructive cycle.

But, for good or for bad, these lessons were carried to Colorado as baggage. I would begin to control myself even more tightly than those who hurt me tried to do.

Indeed, the Tin Woodman began to cry, but fortunately remembered that he might rust, and so dried his tears on Dorothy's apron.

—Oz

This time, instead of the Tin Man, it was Dorothy who cried. Reaching out for Jane's hand, she said, "Good thing I'm not the Tin Man or I would surely rust! And you would have completely rusted when you cried so hard. Now I can't help crying."

"Thank you, Dorothy." What a dear child to accompany me through the pages of my life with such empathy.

"I do want to tell you about my last day in Missouri," Jane interjected. "While we waited for the office to process grades, a colleague and friend took me to a flea market as a distraction. My memory of the day is gray, but her kindness helped me walk through the overwhelming sorrow."

"Oh, how kind," Dorothy said. "Did you buy anything?"

This child's curiosity delighted me!

"Let's see.... I believe my purchase was a children's vinyl record—maybe *Mother Goose.* This may have been the beginning of my collection of records and the reason why lining them up on my office wall in Colorado felt like receiving a warm hug."

"That would make sense, much like my fondness for silver shoes." Dorothy said. "Were things better in Colorado?"

"Yes. It was tough at first, but it did get better and we made many new friends. Those new friends took care of me."

"Oh good," Dorothy said. "Friends are the best part."

"You're right," Jane responded. "And now, we should move on down the Yellow Brick Road to Colorado, because Missouri really did end sadly! I don't like unhappy endings."

No one does.

PART III
COLORADO

This adventure made the travelers more anxious than ever to get out of the forest, so they walked so fast that Dorothy became tired and had to ride on the Lion's back.

–Oz

O h, it's beautiful!" cried Dorothy at first sight of Pikes Peak rising to the west of Colorado Springs.

Non Janyne remembered that she had felt the same way when she first saw Pikes Peak. "Yes, it is beautiful when covered in snow with the blue sky above it. That's how it looked the day Scott drove us to Colorado Springs to begin our new job. Since we needed the income now, I began as an advisor while waiting for full approval for the faculty position opening in the fall. But what a relief to have a job!"

Jane sighed. "I sat and cried when Scott left us to return to Missouri to care for our high school son, and to try to sell our house. Our daughter was finishing her senior year in college in another city. Our family was scattered across the country. This hadn't turned out like we wanted it to."

Dorothy shook her head sadly. "That is how I felt when the Wicked Witch of the West separated me from my companions. For you, Missouri certainly ended sadly, and then you didn't even have the consolation of your family with you."

Everyone sat reflecting for a moment before Dorothy continued. "In Kansas I often imagined a world where the colors were bright and the days were adventurous. It seemed like a dream—but then it happened! I don't think you had many dreams after that sad ending, but did your dream about Washington State begin in Colorado?"

"Yes, it did, Dorothy. The city of Colorado Springs had breathtaking, rugged beauty, but I dreamed of a land with long seasons of luscious green and flowering plants of every color. Colorado Springs was not green enough for me, and it certainly didn't have enough water."

"I can see this is true," Dorothy said. "Maybe Colorado would help you appreciate Washington State more. I know the beauty of Oz sure amazed me, after Kansas!"

> *[It was] a country of marvelous beauty. There were lovely patches of greensward all about, with stately trees bearing rich and luscious fruits. Banks of gorgeous flowers were on every hand, and birds with rare and brilliant plumage sang and fluttered in the trees and bushes.*
>
> –Oz

"Yes, Dorothy, Washington State is as beautiful as the Land of Oz! But wait, you are getting ahead of the story! We still need to tell about Colorado!"

"Oops! I did get ahead of the story." Dorothy laughed at how funny this was after all her efforts to keep the three adults on track.

Colorado would last sixteen years, including three years of intensive therapy. No Wizard could magically bring me the abundant life; but for now, we needed to keep walking toward the Emerald City.

> *'If this road goes in, it must come out,' said the Scarecrow, 'and as the Emerald City is at the other end of the road, we must go wherever it leads us.'*
>
> –Oz

15
THE FIRST TEN YEARS
IN COLORADO

People would rather live in homes regardless of its grayness.
There is no place like home.

–Oz

Dorothy asked, "Did you have a place to live when you got to Colorado?" She remembered leaving her cyclone-delivered house to set out on the Yellow Brick Road. It may have looked old and broken, but it was home.

Janyne, the one who lived with an optimistic outlook no matter what happened, said, "No, our new boss and his family invited us to stay with them while we searched for another place."

Jane fidgeted a bit. "They were kind to us, but crying in the middle of dinner felt awkward. Their son was around our son's age and it made me think about him not being there with me. They understood."

"I agree, that was understandable," Dorothy said. "I missed my uncle and aunt too. At least Toto came with me. But you left your pets behind, didn't you?"

Non Janyne sighed. "Yes; pets and my son. The house needed to be packed and, hopefully, sold. The need to find a place to live loomed over us, along with starting a new job. There were so many problems to solve, but we had a temporary place to stay, and Janyne always approached everything as an adventure."

Janyne laughed. "Like walking under ladders?"

LADDERS AND CAR WRECKS

My first Sunday in Colorado, I attended church at the Air Force Academy. As a sermon illustration, the chaplain placed a ladder in front of the door. I (Janyne) laughed at the superstition and walked under it.... Then, the following week, I had two car accidents. (I still refuse to be superstitious, but ...)

The first accident occurred while driving to my first day of work at the college. Blinded by the intense January sun, I never saw the red light until another car hit me. When the fire truck came, the fireman asked if there was a lot of stress in my life.

Was it that obvious?

Scott's was the only number in my new phone, and he was back in Kansas. But he was able to contact the college for me. When help came, we pulled off pieces of the car's fender so I could drive it ... kind of.

The day felt surreal.

My nice new car, purchased just before everything went south in Missouri, now looked as sad and battered as I felt.

When I finally arrived at work, I found a stack of files waiting for me. The student advisor position, originally an online distance job, now had become an online office job. Navigating a new spreadsheet while reliving the accident throughout the day provided a challenge.... But eventually the day ended.

The second accident, two days later, wasn't my fault.

While I sat at an intersection waiting for the light to turn green and enjoying a full cup of Starbucks coffee, a distracted driver slammed into the back of my car. While I wasn't physically injured, both the back and front of my car sustained damage.... And we never got the coffee stain out of the car's headliner.

This time, I didn't call for help. Arriving at work, the other two online advisors first thought my story of a second wreck was a joke. Realizing the truth, they gathered several others and prayed for me. Then we went outside and tore more parts off my car.

A HAVEN OF SAFETY

After the tumultuous ending of Missouri, and the two accidents, the new college became a haven of rest. I felt like a wounded bird rescued from certain death. My relief was probably similar to Dorothy's when her house landed in Oz. It didn't feel like home, but she was glad to be safe—and those who helped her on her way were kind.

Until Scott returned, new friends provided a place for me to live and recover from months of stress. Their four delightful young boys and I would gather on the couch for reading time as their mother prepared dinner. She often asked me to help with food preparation—until I sliced off the end of my finger with a potato peeler. Then it seemed best for me to just read books.

At night I would shake uncontrollably until falling asleep. I thought maybe Colorado felt colder than Missouri; but in hindsight, I think my body was trying to shake off trauma from the difficult move and two accidents. The piles of blankets provided by my hosts couldn't fully solve the problem.

Eventually, the job became comfortable, the insurance complications from two accidents unwound themselves, and the damage to the car was repaired. I kept smiling, and no one knew my inner struggle that felt like a battle for my life.

⌒

Janyne laughed. "The smile was me! No matter what happened, my smile stood ready, and our life tended to provide good stories to tell. Before long, everyone knew laughter entered the room with me. Telling the story of the ladder from the sermon illustration provided a way to bring lightness out of a heavy situation."

Jane shrugged. "You and Non Janyne didn't want me with you in Colorado. I understood why. We all wanted life in this place to be different."

Non Janyne didn't argue. "Well, we didn't want to do anything to make our new coworkers think there were good reasons for what happened in Missouri. I needed to work hard and find a place for us to live. And we needed Janyne to keep smiling."

THE FAMILY REUNITES

Scott returned two months later with a less than happy teenager, our dog Willie, and two cats (Angel and Max). Our daughter would eventually join us after college graduation.

I rented an apartment and sat on the floor waiting for the truck to arrive. In my absence, Scott sold much of our furniture and decor. Even after all Scott's disposing of things, we discovered we still owned too much stuff for the small, two-bedroom apartment. In addition, I didn't have an office because my (hopefully) temporary position only came with a cubicle. With kind assistance, we rented what would be the first in a long string of storage units.

There's something remarkably comforting about nesting in a new place. Unpacking and decorating felt like Christmas. The apartment, which had recently been renovated after a fire, smelled clean and new (except for a hint of smoke in the kitchen). Young partiers lived upstairs, which made weekends miserable; but with our belongings in place, it felt like home.

My greatest concerns revolved around our children who grew up watching their mother pour her life into career for twenty years then be decimated by the unkind actions of Christian leaders. Such incidences affect families as well. (And our son did have a few rough years ahead.) But we were under the same roof!

We were in this place less than a year before Scott became an apartment complex manager in a different area. The job included an apartment for us—one with the smallest kitchen ever built. Yet, it was comfortable, and no partiers lived upstairs.

~

Non Janyne gave a sigh of pure exhaustion. "We moved so often!'

Janyne and Jane sighed with her.

"My ability to quickly pack up a house became a thing of wonder," boasted Non Janyne.

LIFE MOVES ON

During fifteen years in Colorado, we moved eight times. Our departure from Missouri occurred just before the economic recession hit. Unable to sell our "under water" house, we never bought another. We just kept moving from one place to another attempting to meet our family's ever-changing needs.

Finally, after eight months as an advisor to online students, the faculty position opened for the fall semester. Life began to stabilize—if our life in Colorado ever resembled stable.

During our time in Colorado, Scott worked several jobs before he also found employment at the college. The first ten years were years filled with graduations, marriages, births of grandchildren—and lots of moving.

~

Janyne looked over at Non Janyne. "What you did during those years truly was remarkable. You almost killed us, but your accomplishments did seem beyond possible!"

Non Janyne beamed. "Yes, I agree, they were remarkable."

Jane laughed fondly at Non Janyne then added, "Of course you know your stellarness is likely why I collapsed, right?"

Janyne guffawed at Jane's comeback. "She's correct, you know. Right in the middle of menopause, you decided to complete a dissertation in three months."

"Driven. Absolutely driven," Jane murmured. "Crying during the dissertation committee meeting was awful. Then we broke out with horrible sores all over our body. The dermatologist just held our hands and said he was sorry. The weekly cortisone shots directly in the sores were painful!"

Non Janyne was no longer beaming.

Janyne quickly added, "But you know, Non Janyne, we really are proud of all you accomplished during those years. We still enjoyed our children and grandchildren, all the fun times at work and with friends, and travel with Scott. They were good years—hard but good."

"I agree," Jane said. "We don't want you to ever get so driven again, Non Janyne; but we finally put *Ph.D.* behind our name. It made us all happy. We all fought hard to fulfill that dream!"

Non Janyne beamed again. Then she scowled. "But when we retired, who took our 'Dr. Janyne McConnaughey' name plate off the office door and threw it away, before we even had a chance to save it?"

Jane sighed loudly—this thoughtless and senseless act crossed a boundary of respect and deeply triggered her. But that single act wasn't indicative of all the love and care shown to us at the college for thirteen years. That community proved to be a safe place to prepare for healing.

THE FINAL COLORADO HOUSE

Janyne was eager to talk about her favorite house. "After two apartments and three houses, we landed in the most amazing home!"

"Yes, Janyne, your best adventure yet," Jane said, smiling. "In fact, such a great adventure, that you decided to try writing a whole book about it!"

"Yes, I house sat for several days and typed an entire book manuscript. This one's mine! See, *I* can do stellar things, too."

Non Janyne hurrumphed. "Well, I helped."

Jane laughed. "Yeah, me too."

Dorothy sat forward. "Wait, Janyne, there's another book?"

"Yes, we titled it, *The 4Generation House*. The quirky title was my creation!" And we always called it that; it had a distinct personality and needed a name.

"Did you publish it?" Dorothy was curious now.

"No," Non Janyne lamented. "Not long after finishing the manuscript we began therapy. We didn't have the heart to try to get it published."

"Oh, that's too bad," Dorothy lamented. "What was it about?"

Janyne cleared her throat to stop Non Janyne (still prone to take over) from answering. "It told about the three years Scott and I shared the house with our daughter and her two children while caring for my dad. Of course, since I was the author, it only included happy parts."

"True," Jane said. "Reading your story, no one would imagine we were headed for therapy. My story was completely different."

"You know," Dorothy reflected. "It sounds like the land of Oz. Some places were so happy, but all the while the Wicked Witch of the West lived a totally different life. She probably needed therapy!"

Jane laughed. "I imagine she did. Lots of dysfunctional family stuff in her story."

Dorothy, though, was thinking about the remainder of *this* book. "I have an idea. Why don't you include a chapter from the manuscript you wrote so people know what your life was like during those years?"

At that, Non Janyne could not help but take over. "Great idea! Maybe it will require two short chapters—one about moving in and the other telling some of Janyne's stories."

It was settled.

~

The next two chapters best describe my final gallant efforts to rise above the effects of childhood trauma. The years spent in The 4Generation House were some of my happiest—the calm before the storm. My life at that time held all the markers of abundance. This truth helped me realize I couldn't blame circumstances for my inner turmoil, and positive thinking (or gratitude) couldn't change it.

This house was the place where my dream began—a dream of a future which included enjoying family and friends, traveling, being an author, and contributing to the lives of others in ways not previously imagined.

"That is the dream about the Emerald City of abundant life!" Dorothy proclaimed.

"Yes, Dorothy, I began to define and believe in the possibility without knowing how challenging the path would be. I never considered that the Yellow Brick Road could be so difficult."

Dorothy nodded in agreement. She had never thought so either.

16
LIVING IN
THE 4GENERATION HOUSE

Dorothy shushed everyone. "We can't be interrupting these two chapters. They should be read straight through as Janyne wrote them in *The 4Generation House* manuscript."

The three adults nodded in agreement, though they wondered how it would be possible to not interrupt.

Dorothy shrugged. "OK, if you can't help yourself—but not too much."

"Thank you," the three said in one hushed voice.

MULTIGENERATIONAL LIVING

Our home included three generations until my dad, living alone since my mother's death, came to visit us in Colorado Springs. I asked the family, "What would one more add to this? Do we want my dad to come live with us?"

We all said yes. However, saying yes and accomplishing yes were two different things. I am not sure why contractors build houses with all the bedrooms on the second floor, but we lived in one like that. Going up and down stairs at age ninety-six wouldn't work. We needed to move.

Sharing a house with multiple generations was nothing new to us; moving wasn't either. In fact, we were on move number five since coming to Colorado Springs.

⌒

"I hate moving. Now we were purposefully choosing to move again," interrupted Jane. "You made that choice sound like a calm decision. It wasn't. I was drowning in catastrophic thinking."

Janyne grinned sheepishly. "Sorry, Jane. For me, navigating the confusion was easy."

(The ability to live above chaos with dissociative ease is remarkable.)

~

We would soon be four generations in a house. We moved to Colorado with two generations, two cats, and a dog. We became four generations and one cat.... Oh, and the duck. But first, moving day.

MOVING DAY

We found a great big house with lots and lots of rooms. Along the way, we discovered it is not easy for multiple families to rent a single house. No amount of clarifying our circumstances, the four incomes, or the number of degreed individuals caused the agencies to waver from their "one family only" policy. Finally, a family who found it necessary to leave their dream home understood we weren't a risk!

A phone call came just as we finished loading the truck. My dad had become ill and was admitted to the hospital in Sacramento. At his age (96), this was very serious. We had planned, packed, sold, negotiated, and prayed to make this happen, and now we weren't sure we still had a reason. And so, I collapsed in a heap on the curb in front of a stranger's house and cried out my frustration and concern. With that meltdown over, we continued to move into the great big house we might not need. But after a stay in the hospital and a family-wide logistical planning session, one brother packed our father's belongings in a trailer and pulled it across country, while the other brother arranged a plane flight to transport our elderly father to his new home. Mission accomplished.

On one of the final drives to the house, my daughter and her children arrived with a duckling. I said, "No. Take a picture and find it a home." It was that simple. I felt bad for the little duck who lost its family while crossing the road. This wasn't the happy ending Robert McCloskey wrote in *Make Way for Ducklings*. But a duck added to the household felt like one pet too many.

So, for only one night, we were four generations, a duck, and a very old cat who thought the duck looked tasty. I am sure, though, that the duck lived a peaceful life on the local veterinarian's farm.

And thus we began our adventure.

OF SWINGS, STROLLERS, AND WALKERS

The 4Generation House provided enough space to hold everything the moving truck and my dad's trailer brought—with room to spare. It was certainly a bigger house than any of us ever imagined calling home. The large deck overlooking the golf course, and the recreation center pool provided an additional bonus.

When our granddaughter had joined our family, we had lived in a very small house my parents purchased in Colorado Springs. It was so small, we joked that when the baby arrived—and we put up her swing—someone would have to move out.

In the small kitchen, we could start the dryer, get the silverware, and close the sliding door, all while sitting at the table. The house really was that small. Our family consisted of three adults, a sometimes-visiting son (away at college), a toddler and a soon-to-arrive baby. This precipitated one of our many moves. The baby arrived just as we finished staging the house to sell. Half of what we owned went to storage, but we still needed to live … and the swing inevitably got in the way.

The move from the tiny house to the next more spacious house involved an explosion of swings, strollers, bouncy chairs, toys, and baby furniture. The following move to The 4Generation House (three years later) was the same, except now we traded the swing for a walker—OK, two of them to be exact. When my dad's walker arrived, it wouldn't fit through the door to his bedroom. By this stage in our life we were frequent flyers on Craigslist, where we quickly found another walker—one that *would* go through the doors.

Lifting a stroller or a walker became a common task; they became symbols of our story. One day the walker got away from me and rolled to the middle of the street. Another day, I almost drove away without it. Thankfully, my dad reminded me he needed it.

Though we no longer needed the stroller or the other walker, they stayed long after their usefulness passed. Of course, someone could always find new uses for the no-longer-needed items—like the time our daughter dressed up for Halloween as an old woman and transported our granddaughter through the neighborhood while leaning on Grandpa's extra walker.

A marvelous thing about the great big house with lots and lots of rooms was having two garages, one for cars—three of the four cars, and another for all the other stuff—dangerous. What we no longer used migrated into the fourth garage and vanished until our next move. We would eventually sell the swings, strollers, and walkers (along with other long-forgotten things). Moving would happen again—we knew this would be true. But for the time being, we settled into the house with plenty of room for four adults, two children, a cat, and eventually a dog—but not a duck!

FOUR GENERATIONS AND PETS

The first generation was my dad, otherwise known as Grandpa Jenkins. He grew up on a farm in eastern Colorado, one of six boys and two sisters. His mother worked as a schoolteacher until she married, at which time school policy required that she resign. My dad met my mother when they were both attending college. She became a schoolteacher, and he was a pastor for over sixty years.

The second generation included Scott and me, now called Poppy and Mema. The third generation consisted of our adult children, Melinda (and also Eric and our daughter-in-law Kelly when they came to visit).

The fourth generation included our two grandchildren, Sabien and Aria, who were eight and three, respectively, when we moved into the house.

Then there was Max, the aged cat, and eventually Jirachi, the very anxious Australian Shepherd who would play a prominent role in several of the chaotic events—usually as a result of the doorbell ringing.

The Canada Geese occupying the golf course outside my dad's window provided delightful diversions. While they weren't as plentiful during the final year, during the first two years they were our constant companions.

We learned a lot about geese. We expected them to migrate but learned many didn't leave because of the availability of water and grass on suburban golf courses, city parks, etc. Watching them shake snow off their webbed feet did make one wonder about the wisdom of their choice.

The geese honked loudly when ready to fly. It was their signal to each other and also the signal for us to get to the window and watch them rise into the air and move into formation.

And so, we lived out life as four adults, two children, a very old cat, a soon to arrive puppy and a gaggle of wild geese. Most days were almost ordinary, other days chaotic. Every day provided storytelling material.

FALLING AT A GARAGE SALE

A few days after moving into the house, I fell at a garage sale. While sitting on the ground trying not to cry, I looked up to see a small boy (who lived in the house), standing before me.

"I fell down too," he said sympathetically. "See my owie?"

A marvelous Cars™-themed Band-Aid® covered the worst of the damage on his knee.

"Do you want one?" he asked. "I have more Cars Band-Aids, and I can get you one."

The boy's mother and I exchanged smiles, and she went to the house to retrieve the first aid. The small child continued his care and concern until my knee recovered enough to limp to my car with my Cars™ Band-Aid® and ice pack.

Generally optimistic about my falls, I proclaimed my knee would stop hurting in an hour or so, but this was not the case. In fact, it just got worse, and so we headed to the ER. X-rays indicated no broken bones, but the doctor said, "It's going to hurt more before it hurts less" and prescribed pain pills. I remained optimistic.

As always happens to me when taking Codeine, before long the urge to vomit overcame me. But sitting in my chair with my leg in a brace presented a problem. "Get me something!" I cried.

Scott, in the middle of preparing meatloaf for dinner, grabbed the bowl he just emptied and quickly delivered it to me. What he handed me didn't matter until the episode left me holding a doubly-disgusting bowl.

"What did you bring me?" I asked. "Surely there was something else!"

"Well, you sounded really desperate," he calmly answered.

He had a point.

After the bowl was removed (we may have thrown it away), I sat in the chair and considered how much work still needed to be done in setting up the house. Now what? I limped off to bed, completely unaware the house would soon be the least of my worries!

WHEN THE DOORBELL RINGS

Living in a big house did have its challenges (beyond the cleaning of it). Sometimes we felt too far away from each other. We purchased monitors for the children's rooms and two doorbells for the master suite my father called home.

The doorbells reminded me of a favorite children's book, *The Doorbell Rang.*[29] In the story, a mother is baking cookies, and each time the doorbell rings there arises a new set of problems involving how to divide up cookies among the children. Similarly, whenever a doorbell in the master suite rang, no one knew what might be coming, but it surely would involve problem solving.

The day after my fall at the garage sale, my dad's doorbell rang very early in the morning. He hadn't felt well since his arrival, and now he had lung pain. We eventually realized he had developed blood clots during the plane flight.

Helpless in my knee brace, I watched Scott leave to take my father to the emergency room—the same room and the same doctor who had taken care of me the day before. The doctor said to Scott, "Well, you've had a rough weekend."

After completing the hospital admission process, Scott returned home, drove me to the hospital, procured a wheel chair, and wheeled me to the hospital room my father and I would share for several days.

We have a photo of me sitting in a chair beside my dad's bed with my leg packed in ice. By about the third day, thanks to the excellent care we received, we were taking walks. What a sight: first came the walker, then the old man with a nurse helping him,

---

29. Hutchins, P., *The Doorbell Rang* (Greenwillow Books: NY, 1989).

followed by a woman in a leg brace pulling the oxygen tank.

We spent close to a week in the hospital. My weary body needed this time to read a book, take care of my leg, and rest. But I wouldn't have made the choice voluntarily.

My still-unpacked area of the house remained exactly as left. Once home, though, life began to settle into a routine.

There seemed to be a new story every day! At this point, we had only lived in the house a couple weeks; there was so much ahead of us!

~

Dorothy smiled during the story about the Canada Geese, but refrained from talking until the chapter ended.

"There were lots of geese in Kansas. There weren't any in Oz. There we saw mostly crows, and we needed to protect the Scarecrow. I wonder if the Wizard could have imitated the honk of a goose. He said he could 'imitate any kind of a bird or beast.' He was from Kansas, so probably he could. Too bad he is no longer here to ask."

What fun to have another friend who loved geese. I miss my geese conversations with my dad.

17
TELLING
THE 4GENERATION HOUSE STORIES

'Sit down, please, there are plenty of chairs, and I will tell you my story.'

–Oz

Now it is time to tell your stories about The 4Generation House," Dorothy said. "I will just sit down here and rest a bit while listening. There were probably lots of stories with so many people both young and old living in one house."

"Oh, so many stories," said Janyne. "Life was generally busy in The 4Generation House. But sometimes it was quite peaceful."

"That's right," Jane said. "I remember one evening in particular. I sat in the living room working on my laptop. Scott stood in the kitchen cooking dinner. My dad sat in his favorite chair watching the news and playing games on his iPad. Aria sat at her little table in the living room tearing paper into strips—and occasionally asking for tape for her creations. Sabien was in the basement playing a video game, while his mother worked on a project for National Board Certification. The cat was sleeping somewhere. The dog was watching Scott cook, hoping a delicious morsel would fall to the floor. All seemed peaceful."

"In moments like these, everything worked so well," Non Janyne said. "Of course, it could all change at any moment."

"I found a quote about that," said Janyne, who loved songs and quotes.

The thing about family disasters is that you never have to wait long before the next one puts the previous one into perspective.
–Robert Brault

"What a perfect quote," Dorothy said. Then, in an effort to keep the story moving, she added, "But remember! Don't interrupt as Janyne tells her stories."

The three adult selves looked at each other and shrugged.

LET THE CHAOS BEGIN!

Sometimes chaos came out of nowhere. Things would be moving along fine when some type of space anomaly would occur, and the house seemed to spin out of control. This happened one night when I stepped on Scott's foot. Honestly, I just tried to give him a kiss. His feet are big, and I stepped on one of them—grinding into it even more as I tried to regain my balance.

Just then, we heard eight-year-old Sabien wailing downstairs. Then came a wail from three-year-old Aria and frantic barks from the dog. We moved in the direction of the wailing, only to find Sabien on the floor in the bathroom.

"I fell down and my knee hurts!"

(Dog barking)

"Aria, why are you crying?"

(Dog barking)

"Sabien fell down. (Sob)."

(Dog barking)

"OK, Sabien you are fine. Aria, Sabien's fine."

(Dog barking)

We returned upstairs and, as Melinda dumped a load of clothes on the laundry room floor, Sabien limped up the stairs after us.

"But look, my knee is bleeding."

"Oh, my goodness, it certainly is!" I exclaimed. "Come sit here and we will get band aids."

(Barking dog jumping on Sabien)

"Someone put the dog in the laundry room!" I pleaded.

Melinda interjected, "No, there are clothes on the floor, and he will drag them outside. Put him in the back yard!"

Ahh, there followed a very short moment of calmness. With Sabien bandaged, clothes in the washer, and the dog back in the house, Scott grabbed the trash and headed through the laundry room to the garage.

Crash!

I screamed, then yelled. "What on earth?"

⌒

"It was the scream," Janyne interjected.

Dorothy giggled. "Shush, Janyne. You're interrupting your own story."

⌒

Scott groaned. "I tripped over the dog bone and fell onto the washing machine," he said.

Then the doorbell rang on the TV.

(Dog barking frenzy!)

Aria began to cry.

Somewhat dazed, Melinda tried to capture and calm the dog while I soothed Aria.

Scott made one more attempt with the trash.

GRANDPA JENKINS REMAINS CALM

My dad, who seldom heard the chaos from his bedroom, calmly dozed through such episodes. Sometimes ignorance really is bliss. Unless the family brought the chaos to the bedroom, he simply enjoyed hearing the stories in the aftermath.

His doorbell eventually became a signal for things such as a forgotten paper, another cup of coffee, or—much to my embarrassment—a forgotten meal. Yes, it happened. We joked about it being elder abuse, but it did seem possible I might be getting too old to care for the elderly.

In fact, my dad's quick mind often kept us on track. Soon

after the move, during a doctor visit, they asked me our address. I told them I didn't know. But my father did. From then on, they asked him the questions.

Not that my dad didn't have his moments. One morning he was absentmindedly reading the newspaper when he asked Scott if the paper had come yet.

Scott wasn't exactly sure how to respond. "Uh, Dad, you're reading it."

My father looked down at the paper in front of him and burst into laughter. I reminded him of the time much earlier in his life when he threw his socks in the toilet instead of the hamper. He reminded me of my driver's test at sixteen when I didn't know how to put the brake on and tried to get my foot up on the brake release handle. We both laughed and decided the problem wasn't age.

A WEEK OF STITCHES

One pleasant evening, as winter slipped into spring, the children were playing with the dog in the backyard. The adults, relaxing in the living room, heard a child scream, "He's bleeding!"

With two children in the house, blood wasn't all that unusual, but when Melinda looked outside she saw blood pouring from Jirachi's leg as he frantically tried to lick up the pools of blood already on the deck. Yelling for towels, Scott went into action to wrestle the fifty-four-pound dog to the deck.

The children howled and cried frightened tears over their bleeding dog as I ran for the towels kept for just such emergencies. I stopped and took a picture of the carnage. Who would believe *that much* blood could come out of a dog's leg!

After some effort, the bleeding stopped, and Scott and Melinda set off to the emergency vet. Cleaning the deck and feeding the children became my new priority.

A landscape border did the damage to the dog's leg. The vet said it was a common injury. Who knew? Jirachi came close to needing a transfusion due to the amount of blood he had lost. After surgery, he came home with a cone on his head. And we all collapsed in exhaustion.

ORGANIZING THE CHAOS

People often said to me, "I don't know how you do what you do." Well, me either! The house seemed in constant motion! We juggled lots of balls ... and sometimes we dropped a few.

Running such a large household required a ridiculous level of organization. I kept the schedules in my calendar and every week we sorted it out to make sure everyone and everything was where they or it needed to be at the right time. Hardly a day didn't require shuffling. There were housekeepers, nurses, appointments, repairmen, jobs, workouts, school, church, deliveries, etc. Add to this mix a job that seldom looked the same on any two days, and my life was often mind numbing.

~

Non Janyne involuntarily snorted. Everyone stared at her. "Sorry. But Janyne is making it sound like *she* did all that."

Sheepishly, Janyne confessed, "I know it was you who did it all. But telling the story this way (in singular person) is less confusing for our readers. And it *is* funny, isn't it?"

Dorothy giggled but then looked serious and said, "Shush now."

~

Yes, it all worked, but sometimes my poor brain reached its limit. When this happened, I usually did something awkward. The most uncomfortable moment occurred when the hot water heater stopped working. It was a huge monster of a water heater in the bowels of the basement. One day we had to take cold showers. So we called the owner of the house.

Someone came and temporarily "fixed" it, but soon the cold showers returned. A call came at work. I needed to return home for the repair guys.

We felt the spacious house was worth the half-hour drive to work. Yet, the long drive meant returning home effectively ended my workday. Completing necessary tasks first, I headed out of the office, stopping to tell my male colleague it wouldn't be possible to return until the following day.

"Hey, I have to go back to the house because my hotty-weiter is broken."

A shocked silence hung between us.

"Let me try saying that one more time. My hot … water … heater is broken. The repair guys are coming to fix it."

A relieved expression spread across my colleague's face. We had a good laugh. I headed home, mentally adding *hottyweiter* to the growing list of ridiculous things gifted to me by my exhausted brain that sometimes couldn't speak in coherent sentences.

THE PLACES I HAVE FALLEN

Falling at the garage sale was one of my three falls while living in The 4Generation House. Falling and I have had a long-term relationship. A good friend of mine suffers from the same malady. Our brains do not communicate very well with our feet when we walk. We have fallen into and under trash bins; down and up stairways and hills; across and off stages; in and out of doors; and over and out of chairs. It is remarkable neither one of us ever broke a bone as a result of our many calamities.

The second fall followed ill-chosen words. Melinda called me to ask for an address, so she could send a thank-you card. Both surprised and impressed, instead of giving her praise for sending the card, I responded with, "I better watch my walking today, because the earth just shifted on its axis, and I don't want to fall."

⌣

"Was that you, Non Janyne?" Dorothy asked.

Non Janyne responded with, "Shhh! You are interrupting Janyne's story. But yes; it wasn't an affirming-mother moment."

This time Janyne giggled.

⌣

No more than a half hour later, I ate my words face first on my dad's bedroom floor. There should have been a video of this exquisite fall. Setting his kefir and pills down on a tray, I walked to the window to open the blinds, turned to pick up the tray, and fell over an extension cord (one I had several times made a mental note to move). On the way down, my hand hit the tray sending kefir and pills all over the floor, furniture, and walls.

Enter puppy.

The desperate attempts to keep the puppy from eating the pills and licking the kefir off the walls were awe inspiring. My dad watched in dismay.

When is an accident truly an accident? Not when one has disregarded a potential problem for weeks. Lesson learned.

But the third fall qualified as a true accident.

Scott and I were walking laps around the block after working out. On our final lap, my foot caught on the edge of a landscape border (another landscape border injury). The fall continued in slow motion until my arm and knee went down in the rocks and my head slammed onto the driveway ... while Scott watched helplessly.

Up to this point, my falls had resulted in plenty of minor injuries, but nothing ever broke. A trip to the ER the following day confirmed my luck had run out—my elbow was broken. The bone fragment didn't move, so I thankfully avoided surgery.

This happened on the first day of my summer break and,

just to add to the chaos, the puppy thought my cast looked like a gigantic chew toy waving in the air.

WE SAW FIRE AND WE SAW RAIN

I've seen fire and I've seen rain.
I've seen sunny days that I thought would never end.
–James Taylor

The fall that broke my elbow occurred shortly before my sixtieth birthday. The muscles and tendons injured in the fall were significantly more painful than the elbow itself; saying my arm broke sounded like a more accurate description. Everything became increasingly difficult. It was the beginning of our second summer in the house, and we had great plans—but few came to fruition.

What a relief to be able to remove my half cast to type (and shower) as my arm healed. Before breaking my arm, I had dismantled my office for a redo. Now trying to put it back together—and work in the middle of the mess, with a broken arm—proved challenging.

Then Melinda began to suffer from severe headaches, eventually resulting in two ER visits. One afternoon while Aria napped, I decided to go to work for a few hours. With so little time to work, the office conversations about a fire didn't register. Then my cell phone rang.

"Janyne, are you watching the news? The fire is close to your house!"

Our house sat out on the plains stretching east from the city. There weren't mountains (where most wildfires occured) near the house. I expressed my confusion, and my friend said, "No, it's in Black Forest." My heart sank; I packed up to head home.

While driving down the highway toward home, I could see smoke billowing over our neighborhood. The beautiful forest about two miles from our home was on fire. I listened to the radio, and took pictures at every stop. My mind could not comprehend the enormity of the fire. Just beyond where I turned toward our house, police cars were blocking the road that continued north.

The fire was marching in our direction and the pre-evacuation line enveloped our neighborhood. The chaos of the evacuation from the Waldo Canyon fire the year before was a stark reminder that, besides Scott, we had one bedridden daughter, two small children, one elderly man, a cat, a puppy, and a woman with a broken elbow. This left one able-bodied man in the house. The odds were against us should the fire require us to evacuate.

We took the children to a safe place and our neighbor drove Melinda to the hospital. Scott and I began preparing for evacuation and spent an anxious night before the wind changed direction and turned the fire back on itself. When we knew we were safe, we fell into bed in an exhausted stupor. So many homes burned, and lives disrupted!—a sad day for many.

And then the rain came—the worst thing possible after the fires. But we needed rain—desperately. If the rain had come first, the fire wouldn't have had free reign on the forest. Now rain fell for days, then weeks.

The stories from the summer of fire and rain could fill an entire book; but for now, between the broken elbow, illness, and the fire, we were pretty much done with summer. The following year would be our final year in The 4Generation House.

⌣

Dorothy, who had listened intently to *The 4Generation House* chapters, heaved a sigh of relief when the fire turned from our house.

"The forest is a beautiful place, but it can also be scary," she said.

"You are so right," Janyne responded. "That night I learned the importance of things like fire mitigation. The fire fighters were able to save many houses because of the mitigation work done by owners before and after the Waldo Canyon fire."

"Yes," Dorothy said. "Fire should be respected. The Scarecrow understood this when he said his greatest fear was a lighted match. You probably felt the same."

"I did! Fires are tragic … and exhausting."

"You fell asleep in bed the way I fell asleep on the Lion's back," Dorothy said. "I got tired just listening to the story. What a night!"

Jane sighed. "I do think the exhaustion from that summer may be one reason I began to be overwhelmed with my struggles. It is good that I had a friend to help me. For that reason, we should tell about friendship next."

Dorothy nodded in anticipation. She wished she had the Lion along to lean against instead of a tree. As she waited for the next chapter to begin, she thought of the Scarecrow. She was sure all the talk about the fire would have unsettled him.

18
THE IMPORTANCE
OF FRIENDSHIP

When the Scarecrow found himself among his friends again, he was so happy that he hugged them all, even the Lion and Toto.

—Oz

Smiling at Dorothy, I said, "You could never have made it to the Emerald City without your friends." It was a true sign of friendship that Dorothy had missed the companionship of the Cowardly Lion while listening to the chapters.

"That is so true," Dorothy responded. "I needed the help of my traveling companions."

"Same here, I had many friends over the years and they were all important, but my friend Paula helped me begin my healing journey. She was the one who got me started on the Yellow Brick Road—kind of like the Witch of the North helped you."

"Yes, the Witch of the North helped me get started to the Emerald City. But when you and Paula first met, I doubt if it was because of your house landing on her sister and killing her."

"No, it didn't happen that way!" I laughed (but then wasn't sure I should have laughed). In a more serious tone I said, "Paula was a student in a degree completion program I directed. She also taught theater and music in a local school. We got to know each other as professor and student but became friends after she graduated."

"Oh, that is a much better way to meet!" Dorothy said.

～

My friendship with Paula was perfectly timed. By the third year in The 4Generation House, an indefinable restlessness was rumbling inside me—one I struggled to calm and found impossible to understand. Healing always requires a "coming to the truth" of some sort. No one can heal unless he or she acknowledges their need. For me, this realization began while living in The 4Generation House and enjoying the friendship that would prepare me for therapy.

It's easy to look back and see the pain overtaking me (discussed in the next chapter), but also how my desire to fulfill my early dreams of being an author begged me to begin writing. Many things had prevented the fulfillment of my childhood dream; and reaching that dream would require healing.

I NEEDED A FRIEND

Each friend represents a world in us,
a world not born until they arrive, and it is only
by this meeting that a new world is born.
    –Anais Nin

Janyne glanced over at Non Janyne. "You were very much in control at the time Paula came along. She had to reach around you in order to give Jane and me a hug."

Non Janyne shrugged.

Jane smiled. "Paula helped me believe my life could be different. There was so much pain when she met us."

"I was just excited to break free and enjoy life again." Janyne even now appeared ready to skip away in complete abandon.

Non Janyne sighed. "The loss of control frightened me."

Jane looked sheepish. "It was a bit awkward when I began sharing really sad stuff during dinner on Paula's deck. We'd only come to her house once before—way too early in our friendship for me to puke my soul, but I was primed for the puking."

Janyne, knowing it hadn't been funny at the time, laughed

now. "You just jumped in and started oozing. But Paula was compassionate."

"Yes, always," Jane replied. "There's no greater gift than a friend who believes in us with compassion even when our pain begins to leak through the cracks. I certainly was leaking!"

The compassion received on the deck that night began my journey of healing. This would not be the last time we caught a glimpse of my inner turmoil during the three years we enjoyed close friendship before Paula moved away.

Not having any awareness, at that time, of my internal dissociative structures, I found it difficult to explain my mixed emotions about this emerging friendship. Paula and Janyne were instant friends, but my Jane tendency to "go to the dark side" and my Non Janyne demeanor didn't really fit my Janyne free-spiritedness. So complex to be me!

Paula's house provided a perfect escape from the busyness of The 4Generation House. One night Paula and I heard a performer on a late-night TV show sing a song that included the line, "Take me to the river." Those words prompted unexplainable tears that I didn't understand but couldn't stop. Paula simply went to the piano and began to play as raw pain poured from me in gasping waves.

This gift of music consoled a weeping friend. If she had stayed sitting with me, I would have forced myself to stop crying—but crying was my greatest need. After the torrential release of emotions ran its course, we gave each other a hug, and headed to our rooms for a good night's sleep.

Two years later the repressed memory causing all that pain surfaced, and then the weeping triggered by a song lyric finally made sense. I had been overcome by the traumatized emotions surrounding a date rape as a college freshman that involved being taken to a river.

186

JANYNE TAKES OVER

"I found a compassionate friend who could be trusted," Jane said.

"And I found a co-adventurer," Janyne added. "We walked, hiked, attended the theatre, enjoyed girls' nights, and shared meals together."

Non Janyne, feeling a bit left out, said, "All Paula's accomplishments impressed me. She was a musician, theatre director, teacher, yoga instructor, chef, rock climber and more."

"She also helped me lose the final pounds to reach my 100-pound weight-loss goal," Janyne said—then she sighed, knowing the healing journey had added some of it back.

"Yes," Non Janyne added. "*Her* plan and *my* control did that. Both of you would have cheated."

That was true, but Jane and Janyne still rolled their eyes. Not living under that much control was worth a few pounds.

～

As the weight came off, my transformation wasn't just physical. In hindsight, I now realize the lead person in my dissociative system switched from Non Janyne to Janyne. That changed everything. Paula saw Janyne hidden underneath Non Janyne's control and middle-aged exterior and called her out to play.

My transformation to Janyne caused a rumbling in the force. While Janyne enjoyed the time of her life, Non Janyne sensed the loss of control and often felt terrified by it. Janyne's free-spirited nature no longer seemed like a good fit at the college, and she began to apply for other jobs. This disturbed Jane because of the experience in Missouri. But Janyne had finally tasted freedom and wanted to try greener fields.

During this transition, Scott and I travelled to Missouri for a funeral, and many of my long-time acquaintances there didn't immediately recognize me. A friend said, "Janyne, you were always a nice-looking woman, but I would never have described you as cute. But now you are." Janyne liked that!

More than just losing weight, the change involved my mannerisms, self confidence, and expressions. Since personality changes are common when people lose such a significant amount of weight, I simply enjoyed the compliment and didn't think much of it.

~

Dorothy tapped me on the shoulder. "Wait, you said you didn't change how you looked, but now you say you did."

She made a good point. "Well, I still looked like me and didn't turn into a fairy princess or wizard like Oz did. I was myself but somehow different. People attributed it to the weight loss, but the real difference was feeling like an entirely different person inside. Oz still felt like Oz; only his appearance changed. Conversely, my feeling different inside made me change on the outside. Does that make sense?"

"It does," Dorothy answered. "When the Lion felt courageous, he appeared very different from the fearful lion he'd been."

"Perfect example, Dorothy! It really was all based on feelings or the lack of them. Janyne's emotions were completely different from the other two, and she started flying solo."

UNDERNEATH JANYNE

Despite this transformation, the side of me that continually expected the other shoe to fall was evident to my friend. She did her best to counter it with her own positive attitude, but something in me (Jane) knew the other shoe would eventually crush her (Now understood as well-founded catastrophic thinking and hypervigilance).

Not long before the fall that broke my elbow, Paula needed emergency surgery. Since her husband was out of the country, I became her support person. Arriving at the hospital to drive her home and seeing everything that needed carrying, I suggested, "Why don't I go ahead and take the flowers to the car while we wait for the attendant to bring the wheelchair for you."

The flowers consisted of five fabulous bouquets. In typical fashion, my carefully-hidden hypervigilant mind imagined every possible scenario on the way to putting the flowers in the car.

There was a concern. "I hate to leave them unattended in the loading area while going for the car."

"Janyne, just leave them at the loading area. Who's going to mess with flower arrangements?" said Paula.

"You're right. Just me going to the dark side."

Now mind you, these were no ordinary flower arrangements. They became the topic of conversation in the hallway, in the elevator, and throughout the lobby.

"What kind of flowers are those?" people asked.

Am I a florist? was my unspoken thought. I was uncomfortable being the center of attention while rolling a cart of flowers of which I knew not the identity.

In the few moments it took to get the car and return to the loading area, my worst-case scenario materialized. Two older women stood pulling flowers from the arrangements and even tipped over a bouquet, spilling water everywhere.

Approaching the women, I hinted, "Aren't my friend's flowers beautiful?"

"Oh, are these yours? We thought someone who didn't want to take them home left them here," said the woman with the hospital volunteer badge.

Did people discard beautiful flowers at the loading area on a regular basis? Not likely, yet these flowers were tempting and had been left completely helpless and vulnerable!

The flowers were safely in the car by the time the attendant wheeled my friend to the loading area. My telling of the story ended with, "Sometimes there's predictive value in my propensity for going to the dark side." I (Jane) felt vindicated.

So much hypervigilance. Not even Janyne's dominant free-spirited personality could suppress or hide this tendency. Honestly, it appeared to be a super power—an exhausting and irritating one.

Paula helped me to realize not everyone constantly scanned for potential disaster; it was neither healthy nor necessary. This revelation surprised me, since I believed these complicated strategies were how everyone lived.

TRYING TO RELAX

While enjoying being Janyne, the underlying inability to relax remained. Paula thought yoga would be a good way to help me. With my elbow now sufficiently healed, she suggested restorative yoga.

My immediate overpowering fear of yoga seemed almost pathological and somehow connected to my mother. This felt awkward; but certainly, she would have disapproved. It confused me. Why would my deceased mother's approval for yoga be necessary? In addition, I couldn't imagine trying to get my body to understand what it needed to do, with people sitting on mats all around me.

There was also an illogical fear my faith was ill-equipped to prevent me from adopting beliefs from eastern religions. Understanding Christianity's roots weren't Western anyway persuaded me to give yoga a try. So much angst over every choice!

To my surprise, my yoga instructor was Jewish. The class included a mix of traditions and provided a much-needed mind-body connection. Yet, the idea of totally relaxing terrified me. It felt as disturbing as my struggles with extended times of silent prayer. Any form of relaxation brought uncomfortable feelings, emotions, and body sensations.

I eventually read an explanation of this by Dr. Bessel Van der Kolk, leading trauma researcher: "Traumatized people often are terrified of the sensations in their own bodies. Most trauma-sensitive people need some form of body-oriented psychother-apy or bodywork to regain a sense of safety in their bodies."[30] Once again, something I had thought was "just me," wasn't. It was a product of trauma.

Yoga played an important role in preparing me for therapy. The emphasis on breathing exposed my shallow breaths. Learn-ing how breathing calms anxiety would prove valuable.[31] Yoga also enabled me to "connect" to my body and feel the physical sensations ignored for a lifetime.

I suggest trauma-informed yoga classes to survivors. Increas-ingly, therapists are including yoga as part of their practice or as a recommendation. Without having participated in yoga before beginning therapy, when asked to identify the locations of feel-ings or pain, I would have said, "In my head."

Healing depended on identifying and accepting feelings as sensations in my body! The body sensations felt uncomfortable when relaxing during yoga, so I had no problem identifying the location of the feeling as therapy began.

---

30. "Yoga and Post-Traumatic Stress Disorder, An Interview with Bessel van der Kolk, MD" is available at http://www.traumacenter.org/clients/MagInside.Su09.p12-13.pdf . Additional resources on the topic are available at the website for The Trauma Center at Justice Research Institute: http://www.traumacenter.org/products/publications.php .

31. Zimmerman, E., "I Now Suspect the Vagus Nerve is the Key to Well-Being" *Science of Us* (May 9, 2019) retrieved from: https://www.thecut.com/2019/05/i-now-suspect-the-vagus-nerve-is-the-key-to-well-being.html?utm_campaign=sou&utm_source=fb&utm_medium=s1&fbclid=IwAR1NUsRzA0KXjQGZOjcSo08hADrtOJTjfv47B_5WdBChvFMo3AezqJVNANQ

FOLLOWING THE DREAM

Paula's introduction of yoga helped Jane learn to recognize feelings as sensations within the body, but Janyne was most inspired by watching her friend dream big dreams.

"Paula helped us dream and know we could follow our dreams. This was when we decided to write *The 4Generation House,* and begin a blog."

Non Janyne, the one who knew how to put a plan in motion, said, "Paula's house was empty for several days and we house sat with Lucy the cat and Champ the loveable Labrador.... And Janyne wrote. Within just a few days, the book took form, along with several blog posts."

Yes, Non Janyne could create a plan and put it into action.

Janyne continued, "Part of this process required deciding on a platform for my website. What would I say? I was dreaming; but Non Janyne's determination often stepped in and started writing. Here is one example:"

I have always believed thinking was the key. One of my treasures is a vinyl recording of The Little Engine that Could. *We all know the story but probably best remember the line, "I think I can, I think I can."*

Henry Ford said, "If a man thinks he can or thinks he can't, he is right." I agree and have proven this in my life—both ways. Accomplishments happen because I think I can do it. Acknowledging God's strength and help does us no good unless we "think we can!" So many dreams die inside our heads. I am one determined person; but I believe every person has the potential to reach his or her dreams. Self doubt is the enemy of accomplishment.

Janyne giggled. "Notice it's all about thinking?"

"No, you wouldn't consider emotions, would you?" Jane responded.

Feeling the tension in the air, Janyne decided to move the conversation in a new direction. "Paula's positive thinking continued to influence me during the most intense months of therapy. It helped me believe it would be possible to come out on the other side and access abundant life."

"I agree," Non Janyne said. "I embraced this belief and worked to heal with untiring determination."

Jane sighed deeply before adding, "And I learned that someone could be fully trusted not to reject my pain. This would eventually help me be willing to seek help."

~

Dorothy, clearly excited, jumped up from where she was seated. "You are right! Paula really was like the good Witch of the North. She came out of nowhere and helped you know how to get to the Emerald City."

"She did exactly that! And eventually she would send me on my way with a blessing, just like the Witch of the North did for you. If Paula had stayed with me, or if the Witch of the North had stayed with you, neither of us would have ever understood how brave we really were."

> *'Won't you go with me?' pleaded the girl, who had begun to look upon the little old woman as her only friend.*
> *'No, I cannot do that,' she replied, 'but I will give you my kiss, and no one will dare injure a person who has been kissed by the Witch of the North.' She came close to Dorothy and kissed her gently on the forehead.*
> *–Oz*

19
THE APPROACHING STORM

Dorothy could see where the long grass bowed in waves before the coming storm. There now came a sharp whistling in the air from the south, and as they turned their eyes that way they saw ripples in the grass coming from that direction also.

–Oz

We felt the storm approaching." said Janyne, who didn't usually acknowledge turmoil. But the approaching storm during the last year in The 4Generation House had been unsettling even to her.

"I did my best," Jane responded.

"We all did," Non Janyne added with a sigh of resignation. "We blamed you, Jane, because you began to leak. I tried to control it, but that task became more and more difficult."

"True," Janyne said. "And then I took over Non Janyne's role as the one who stepped forward to live life. But being in charge and controlling things is not one of my strengths."

At that Non Janyne and Jane both laughed in agreement. Then Non Janyne grew serious. "The truth is, no amount of control could last forever. Control couldn't be the answer; it was just the best we could do most of our life, up until then. I wish we could have understood what was going on, how our controls were collapsing. We needed help. Not just you, Jane; we all needed help."

"True," Jane said. "This storm brewed for years deep inside me; and we came to the place where you two just couldn't help me any longer. We loved our family and wanted to be there for them. But the stress of living in a house with so much happening, became overwhelming."

WATCHING THE APPROACHING STORMS

Caring for my dad was a fulfilling and consuming task that played an important part in my preparation for therapy. We built our father-daughter relationship on the foundation of caring for each other. The care our family provided for him became my ultimate subconscious thank-you for how his love enabled me to survive my childhood pain.

The days we spent building a ramp for him to navigate in and out of the house would eventually help me find the small child self inside me who surfaced during therapy, and who had "used the hammer" to "board up" oozing memories. The time spent building the ramp together played a vital role in preparing to reframe my childhood story with both good memories and painful truths.

Scott and I grew weary from the long drive to and from work. The constant activity in the house, the required upkeep, and my dad's increasing need for care, took a toll on us also. Our greatest concern became our inability to monitor him closely while working so far from home. Scott began going home at lunch to check on him, causing his daily driving time to increase to two hours a day.

We gave the local fire department the code to access the house, and my father agreed to wear a fall alert. I started working from home more often; and eventually, on the days I went to the office we hired a friend to come and make lunch for him. But still concerned, we had the feeling the storm we felt coming was going to be the upheaval of providing adequate care.

My dad and I talked about weather quite often. Having grown up at the eastern edge of Colorado, he told me many weather-related stories. During spring in Colorado, the weather can change multiple times in a day. A sunny day can turn stormy in an astonishingly short amount of time as the storms come over the Rocky Mountains. Pikes Peak would vanish, and soon distant thunder would rumble.

My emotions during those last few months in The 4Generation House mirrored those rolling, passing storm clouds. My sunny disposition would turn dark with deep inexplicable pain. Rotating between happy, sad, determined, stalled out, overly optimistic, and depressed, I spiraled. But I attributed it to stress.

THE UNKNOWN

Uncertainty about the future added tension to our lives. The thought of packing again, along with the decisions about where to move, overwhelmed me. Some days I thought the answer might be to find another job while my dad could still travel to another city. But if we stayed in Colorado Springs, we needed to live closer to work. And if we moved into town, should we move into separate homes? Then the news came.... My friend might also be moving.

I both dreaded and desired change.

One October night, a year before walking into therapy, I typed an e-mail to Paula expressing my inability to remain positive about life. I was prompted to write to Paula by a comment one of my students had written:

> *I now understand that it is not just providing [students] information, but there are times we have to help them undo knowledge that they constructed based on what they already knew but was a misconception. [sic] We cannot just tell them they are wrong and give them new information, we must help them reconstruct their knowledge.*

This student comment about disequilibrium caused an epiphany for me: I could never change something deep inside me simply by trying. After a lifetime of repression and of trying to control and change—this truth finally sank in.

My e-mail to Paula revealed my struggles:[32]

I know I just continually go to the dark side about my future, but I can't seem to shake it. I just keep going there. I know this verse in my head: 'I know the plans I have for you,' declares the Lord, 'plans to prosper you and not to harm you, plans to give you hope and a future.'

It is deeply ingrained in my spirit that the plans God has for me are just some type of character building journey where life is continually less than what I hope for ... and difficult. I just have to trudge ahead with what God has given me and make the best of it. Nothing I hope for will ever fully happen. I can't just tell myself I am wrong. I have to somehow reconstruct my knowledge—my very view of those 'plans that God has for me.'

My journey to *BRAVE* began in the final sentence:

But if God does have something ahead of me, I will totally miss it unless I can reconstruct how I view God and life.

My searching over the next few months helped me recognize that God did want good things in my future. My struggles were not "God's plan."

32. My level of turmoil in these e-mails is evident in the excessive use of the pronoun "I." This is true in my process writings. Zimmermann, J., Wolf, M., Bock, A., Peham, D., Benecke, C., "The Way We Refer to Ourselves Reflects How We Relate to Others: Associations Between First-Person Pronoun Use and Interpersonal Problems," *Journal of Research in Personality* (Volume 47, Issue 3, 2013, Pages 218-225). Retrieved from: https://www.sciencedirect.com/science/article/abs/pii/S0092656613000160?via%3Dihub

ATTEMPTS AT A BETTER FUTURE

The emerging belief that it might be possible to have a better future prompted me to pursue a different job—in earnest. While grateful for the refuge the current college had provided after Missouri, changes had occured since then—changes both in this college and in me. I felt my time at this college in Colorado was coming to an end. My experience in Missouri warned me not to dismiss the now-familiar feeling.

I began applying for positions at several large Christian universities. In hindsight, I feel badly for those who tried to hire me and found themselves unable to do so because of unforeseen circumstances or complications. They all voiced their disappointment.

～

Jane interrupted. "We tried to change our circumstances. This is what survivors do when the turmoil begins to overcome them. Our mother always wanted to move when things weren't perfect. But we needed to stay put in Colorado Springs. This time healing required us to stay put."

Non Janyne nodded. "Not that God couldn't have figured out another path of healing, but we are glad it was Dr. Sue who helped us."

"Yes, we are," Jane and Janyne said. And in the background, a chorus of children's voices echoed in agreement.

THE ROOTS OF UNWORTHINESS

Jane was right. My search for relief from the turmoil could have resulted in unconsciously repeating a generational pattern and dragging my father with me—just as my mother had often done before me.

But, while leaving Colorado Springs would not have changed anything, staying didn't feel positive either. In fact, it felt as if God might have good futures for others, but not for me. Not that it wasn't possible; I just didn't believe it could happen for *me*. This sense of unworthiness was overpowering, even if inexplicable and illogical. No amount of problem solving could help me understand my feelings. Understanding would have required me to access repressed memories. My inner searching during these months helped me think differently about God but did not address the underlying emotions or touch the internalized messages of shame.

Actually, knowing the truth of my story still might not have helped. Many say they *understand* what happened to them, but it doesn't change how they *feel*. I empathize with them because, like my own, the roots of unworthiness may not be consciously known. I came to this realization while reprocessing a childhood memory during therapy. What actually happened, it turned out, was different from the way I had always remembered and told it.

It happened one Sunday morning in Sunday School when my nine-year-old self refused to sing "Jesus Loves Me." The "cover story" I had always told later, to hide the truth from even myself, was that I refused to sing the song because it bored me. The following cognitive retelling that I wrote after an EMDR therapy session in which I revisited that memory, explains what actually happened:

> *I am in a classroom at church. Our chairs are lined up in a half circle and we are standing and singing. I am not singing. I am standing there watching the others sing. They are singing, 'Jesus loves me, this I know, for the Bible tells me so.' I am not singing—because it isn't true, and the Bible doesn't tell me anything. Singing would be lying, because it's not true. I always tell the truth and am not going to sing a lie. I know I'm not like everyone else. There is something wrong with me. I feel things where I shouldn't. I'm different. I feel dark inside.*

*I don't know what that feeling is. It has always been there.
I have always felt like this, but I don't know why. The teacher
is asking, 'Jeannie, why aren't you singing?' I answer, 'We sing
this song every Sunday. I don't want to sing it anymore!'*

The memory continued, bringing with it waves of shame.
The teacher said she would tell my mother about my refusal to
sing. That possibility terrified me.

Then the pain exploded, and the memory ended with this
self declaration:

*I feel the darkness inside me. I know I have feelings I
shouldn't have. I'm bad. I'm bad.*

LIVING WITH SHAME

"God couldn't love such a bad child" became the root of my
unworthiness. My nine-year-old self needed to tell her story to
trusted and wise adults who could help her reframe the incorrect internalized messages of shame. Since that did not happen,
Nine (my nine-year-old child self) simply accepted that she was
unworthy of Jesus' love.

By the time Ten went to camp the next year, her shame was
already deeply layered, and it only took one adult's "flinch" to
trigger her feelings of unworthiness.

Asking for God's forgiveness didn't and couldn't heal the
childhood pain and internalized messages. When I didn't seem
to feel the way others appeared to feel when they asked for forgiveness, I believed Jesus didn't love me the same as he loved
them.

By my middle adult years, shame didn't even register as
something that affected me. I had built protective structures
around my sense of shame and worthlessness. My disconnected
state, during that period of time in Colorado, felt true to how
my life had always been. My repressed shame didn't feel like the

self loathing experienced by many survivors. Instead, it seemed like the joy others experienced was something outside of my reality. Especially when a storm was approaching.

∽

Jane sighed in relief. "I didn't understand any of this. I just felt a darkness that terrified me. This storm felt bigger and stronger than any before it."

Janyne sighed. "I felt I had to keep living above the pain you carried, Jane, and continue making memories and hoping for the future."

Non Janyne added, "All that time I was enjoying my new Instructional Design position at the college, because my expertise in teaching was finally acknowledged and utilized."

∽

Absolutely true. Jane was becoming increasingly inconvenient to Janyne and Non Janyne's life and plans.

These three different life perspectives couldn't sit in the same space and therefore rotated through my life like a revolving door threatening to spin out of control. But on the surface, no one could have known that a storm was brewing—it was a desperately hidden truth. If anyone asked me, life was great … just busy. Storms had overtaken me before; surely this one would pass.

∽

The three adults, still in conversation, moved on to the next chapter, providing an opportunity for Dorothy and I to talk together.

Dorothy began: "You were familiar with storms. I wasn't. Yet, during the cyclone, I got used to the wind shrieking about me."

"Yes, you even went to lie down on the bed. You inspired me by your calmness. We can become so accustomed to storms, though, that we think they are normal. Some are; but mine weren't.... Listen to how calm you acted:"

*Hour after hour passed away, and slowly Dorothy got over
her fright; but she felt quite lonely, and the wind shrieked
so loudly all about her that she nearly became deaf. At first
she had wondered if she would be dashed to pieces when the
house fell again; but as the hours passed and nothing terrible
happened, she stopped worrying and resolved to wait calmly
and see what the future would bring.*

–Oz

Dorothy smiled now. "I did feel calm. It didn't do me any
good to fret about the future. A tornado spinning my house
like that was so unexpected that it was impossible to know what
would happen next. Whatever was going to happen would just
happen, but it did frighten me when Toto fell through the hole
in the floor."

Dorothy and I considered this a moment and then hugged
our dogs, Toto and Weber. Staring off into the distance, my
mind could imagine the storm approaching. This time, it wasn't
going to be possible to simply let it pass.

20
LIVING ABOVE THE STORM

It was very dark, and the wind howled horribly around her, but Dorothy found she was riding quite easily. After the first few whirls around, and one other time when the house tipped badly, she felt as if she were being rocked gently, like a baby in a cradle.

–Oz

Dorothy and I continued talking as we caught up with the adult selves. "During the storm, you were rocked in the wind like the baby in the cradle in the nursery rhyme," I reminded her.

> *Rock-a-bye baby, on the tree top,*
> *When the wind blows, the cradle will rock,*
> *When the bough breaks, the cradle will fall,*
> *And down will come baby, cradle and all.*

I showed her the picture in the book of *Nursery Rhymes* carried with me since childhood. True, sometimes the wind can rock a cradle gently, but my precarious mental situation seemed much like the baby hanging in the tree. Though Albuquerque wasn't an overly windy city (in comparison to Colorado) the occasional high winds concerned me as a child and made me wonder why the baby's mother hung her in a tree. The wind was certainly not always gentle.

The three adults knew this to be true about wind. One day after a fierce Colorado windstorm, I drove over to check Paula's house and found her gazebo in a mangled heap.

"Dorothy, now that you are traveling with me, it amuses

me that I texted Paula to say Godzilla had visited her deck and some of her belongings might be in Kansas."

Dorothy giggled. "Maybe my aunt and uncle have them."

"They may also have a chair cushion from our front porch in Washington!" We laughed, but we understood the damage storms can sometimes cause.

Jane sighed. "I do miss both decks—Paula's and the one on The 4Generation House. We all loved a deck with a view."

Non Janyne agreed with Jane. "That's why we bought deck furniture the very first day."

Jane smiled. "Nothing calmed me more than sitting on the deck and watching Colorado sunsets."

CANOPY IN THE TREETOP

Sunsets were beautiful, but during the day the sun's intensity became uncomfortable. My Non Janyne adult self had solved the problem by purchasing a canopy to shield us. The deck, my favorite place, held so many memories: sitting and gazing at the stars, watching a movie in the evening, talking with friends, and eating meals together.

My heart still longs for that deck. But one night a storm came across the mountains with a house-shaking wind. Standing at the window, we watched our canopy fly up, up into the air and land upside down in a treetop.

We didn't have the heart to replace the twisted, broken canopy. The deck never felt the same after that, though. The canopy in the treetop on that dark, stormy night provided a metaphor of how hard I worked to bring positive things into my life only to have them destroyed by storms. The other shoe had fallen once again.

Non Janyne, who didn't always feel emotions, did remember how discouraging it was to see the canopy in the treetop.

"Stupid wind," she said.

Jane smiled at this unusual display of emotion as Dorothy added, "Those were my exact feelings when realizing my house wasn't in Kansas anymore."

SEARCHING FOR CLUES

Losing the canopy was frustrating but not the worst of my problems. The storm outside paled in comparison to my inner storm. My deep despair is evident in the numerous documents I wrote at the time and saved on my laptop. One described my lifelong attempt to understand Paul's thorn discussed in Second Corinthians. I still believed the problem to be the "thorn of depression." My writing inadvertently described Jane and Janyne:

> I connected Paul's thorn with 'the sin that doth so easily beset.' Sin isn't even in there, though. Instead it is a picture of the amazing victory and lowest ebbs of someone who struggles. What is that struggle? I have no idea what Paul's was, but I know my own. I am two people. Today I am the person who pleads with God to remove my genetic predisposition to depression. I look out of this wallow to that other person who flies above the clouds, believes anything is possible, and walks on water to get there. When I am her, I do not know the person I am today. When I am this person, I can still see 'the other' in paradise.

In 2014, with all the advances in understanding the effects of trauma, I still did not have access to the information which could have helped me understand my suffering. Believing this problem to be genetic gave me no hope of healing. Fifteen years after writing *Waiting for a Brain Transplant*, I still believed depression was the result of a genetic predisposition.[33] How sad.

~

Dorothy listened with concern on her face and then gave me a hug. "Just like the Cowardly Lion, you thought you were born that way." She picked up her book and read:

'What makes you a coward?' asked Dorothy, looking at the great beast in wonder, for he was as big as a small horse.
'It's a mystery,' replied the Lion. 'I suppose I was born that way.'

–Oz

I agreed. "Something must have happened to him as a young cub to make him afraid. He wasn't born to be afraid any more than I was born to be depressed. Terrible things happened to me—and who knows, maybe to the Lion also!"

Jane sat quietly reflecting. "The pain leaked into my e-mails to Paula."

Non Janyne sighed. "It became impossible to stop you from hitting *send*. My control didn't work anymore. But now I understand you were crying for help."

CRYING FOR HELP

A few e-mails were strangely ominous. One dark night, the following rambling e-mail arrived in Paula's inbox:

---

33. My mother and I both suffered from depression and probably experienced similar trauma. Genetic and/or epigenetic factors may have been involved, but healing ended my suffering described in this chapter. While this may not always be the case, it convinces me that genetics may have contributed, but did not cause the depression. New research is unfolding every day on the body/mind connection and the interplay between factors which include childhood adversity, epigenetic expression of DNA, the vagus nerve; and most recently the imbalance of gut bacteria as a symptom (not identified as a cause) of depression.

I have heard of two instances of people in ministry taking their own lives. How does this happen? I know how it happens—it is living the life with the 'game face' and finally just coming apart. It happens by suicide (most tragically), by catastrophic moral failure, or dropping out of ministry and vanishing into a pit of misery. All three of those have been in my thoughts over the years, and I don't believe I am alone in this. I had it all under tight control, but our friendship made me vulnerable and I've been trying to get the control back. I had an argument with God about this. I said, 'It was better for me to be that other person and able to control the degree to which I am willing to be vulnerable.' I am out of control, hurting, back to the darkness, unable to check my emotions, unable to wrap the wall of protection around me again. My old self is calling me back with the lure of controlled security.

～

"You *wanted* me back in control?" Non Janyne asked.

"Yes. We needed you!" Jane and Janyne both exclaimed.

Jane added, "Your straight-to-the-point voice and controlling ways often give you a bad image in our writing but you were the reason we lived life as a functional person."

Janyne agreed and then glanced at the remainder of the e-mail. "I wrote this next part to Paula because Jane kept stepping in and ruining my enjoyable life."

Over the years we have been friends, I have very carefully guarded this part of me. As vulnerable as I have been, I was not going to let you know about this 'crazy' inside of me. For the past month, I have felt my outer layer of protection cracking and crumbling, and it is like my insides are oozing out. As soon as I check one spot, some other support structure fails, and I am doing damage control somewhere else. I am just about as fragile as I have ever been in my life. It absolutely terrifies me.

Janyne glanced at Jane apologetically. "It wasn't your fault. But the way you sent these e-mails and then showed up as a happy person undoubtedly confused Paula."

Jane shrugged. "No one wanted *me* around. They loved your laugh. You didn't even remember the cliff, but I did. In the next e-mail I stepped in and described what happened."

There is a fine line between sane and crazy in the world of Janyne. I was really afraid yesterday because I knew I was crossing the line to crazy and was just pleading for help. You probably prayed for me. Last night I fell off a cliff and was just grabbing at any branch I could find on the way down. I haven't frightened myself like that in a long time. I lived in the darkness for years. That's why I went on meds. I watched my mother live in crazy her whole life. I don't ever want to go there again, it terrifies me. I feel relieved but not better, yet. I can't even function right now. Scott may just have to send me somewhere.

Janyne looked shocked. "No way! I had no conscious memory of the cliff experience of my young adult self, but I managed to describe it anyway. And during therapy I did a lot of talk about falling off cliffs. But when writing this, it just felt like the very earth began crumbling underneath me as I desperately tried to grab onto hope on the way down."[34]

The three sat quietly pondering how well the e-mail described the cliff experience that later, during therapy, returned to my conscious memory.

---

34. This is an example of an emotional flashback—sudden overwhelming emotions—without an identifiable cause. While writing the e-mail, I described what happened and felt the emotional distress without consciously remembering the experience. My subconscious, protective coping mechanisms were strong.

~

There was nothing in my current life warranting such deep turmoil. Without consciously remembering the cliff, my thoughts in the e-mail appeared torturous, but not dangerous. Only when the memory of the cliff surfaced did I recognize the suicidal thoughts embedded in my words.

These e-mails reveal the greatest danger of depending on dissociative coping mechanisms to survive. It is completely possible to not be aware that you are living in two or more emotionally different worlds. Would Janyne or Non Janyne have ever considered suicide? Absolutely not! Janyne was enjoying life. Non Janyne was judgmental toward anyone who had such "selfish" thoughts. But Jane held the pain of everything I shared in *BRAVE* ... and more. And now the Jane part of me could no longer hold the pain, and she was trying to figure out how to escape.

Paula remained steady as these e-mails oozed the pain hiding deep within me. So often, our inclination is to step back, put up guards, or walk away from those whose deep emotional material is leaking out in public ways. Her response was nonjudgmental love. Neither of us understood why this miserable "me" sent those e-mails. I'm thankful my friend never flinched.

WHERE DO WE TURN?

In hindsight, either my friend or my husband probably should have "sent me somewhere," but my dissociative ability to move in and out of this dark place and appear fine made it more like an anomaly than a daily truth.

When I read headlines of tragic suicides, my heart hurts for the loved ones who mistakenly believe that if they could have or would have done something differently, the result would have been different. The ones who feel this way are most likely those who did care and were trying to help. The research says that the one way we make a difference it to be a non-judgmental and calm presence, but even this comes without guarantees.

We can hold space for others, encourage them to seek help, even find help for them; but suicide can still occur. By the time my car turned up the mountain road, I was beyond the point of consciously making decisions. The need to escape the excruciating mental and physical anguish consumed me. The best time to seek help would have been many years before that point.

Yet I miraculously lived, but with the memory of deep anguish still inside me; and now it was surfacing. Outside of this friendship, where could I have turned to express these emotions? How can I explain the pressure being a professor at a Bible college placed on me? Where do church members or leaders within Christian ministries feel safe to share such deep inner turmoil?

I had finally come to understand that the problem wasn't spiritual, and my intuition said to not risk anyone telling me differently. The possibility of someone quoting scripture to me after years of teaching verses to my students and children seemed like a risk I dared not take.

The pressure to disguise and hide our inner pain is killing those of us who, like myself, cannot reconcile the darkness with our sincere desire to live the abundant life Jesus promised. Some of us are living with stress or trauma-related physical illnesses that will eventually kill us; or in the worst-case scenario, we are contemplating ways to finally end the pain.[35] We certainly are not living the abundant life; but our words, spiritual fervor, and Facebook posts tell others a different story.

---

35. Suicidal ideation is a common struggle for trauma survivors. See Addendum 4, Suicide Prevention Resources, and seek help if you are struggling. National Suicide Prevention Lifeline: Call 1-800-273-8255

HOW TO MAKE A DIFFERENCE

A friend with a story of childhood abuse much like mine went to see a person she identified as a "spiritual counselor" and shared her troubled emotions along with some of her story. In response to her sharing, she was told that her anxiety and feelings of unworthiness were sinful. This church staff member had the best intentions but lacked an understanding of the effects of trauma. In my own turmoil, receiving this type of response could have resulted in tragic consequences.

It is essential to tread carefully as others express deeply troubling emotions. When Christians who are doing their best to live a wholesome life and serve God, share deep emotional turmoil mixed with spiritual doubts, it is most likely rooted in painful childhood experiences. Sometimes, as in my case, the emotional distress doesn't appear to have a cause.

The role of pastoral counseling should be to hold space for these individuals and help them feel comfortable with seeking professional care. Be cautious about digging around for the hidden story! Opening trauma wounds without first establishing containment strategies can be perilous. This is the work of trained professionals.

Encouraging a person to open a wound is a sacred responsibility. Asking someone to be vulnerable and then rejecting them for their over-sharing or "neediness" is all too common—and dangerous. As Ten learned, not all who care are ready to hear the truth.

It encourages me when individuals begin learning about the effects of trauma, recommending my books or other resources, and helping those who share their stories of trauma to seek professional help—specifically, EMDR therapy. This was the case after my friend returned to the counselor's office to explain how painfully off target her words had been.

Becoming trauma informed helps everyone walk alongside

survivors, understand the process of healing (which is usually very messy), establish compassionate boundaries, and provide unconditional support. Healing requires a village.

IT WASN'T WEAKNESS

Even when survivors of childhood sexual abuse struggle, they are the strongest people you will ever meet. The fact they are still alive proclaims this truth. Those who have chosen healing deserve our greatest respect and support.... Stand in awe of them! They need your unconditional and nonjudgmental support. Many with stories like mine, don't fare so well. The adults who loved and supported me during my childhood made all the difference, but this doesn't change the fact that most of my suffering wasn't necessary. A trauma-informed world could have stopped the train wreck at so many points. Trauma-informed parents could have allowed me to cry, a doctor could have recognized the effects of ACEs, employers could have reacted with compassion, and the church could have told me the problem wasn't spiritual. But none of this happened.

⁓

Dorothy stood before me offering a tissue. "You need to cry like the Tin Man did. Remember how he came to me?"

'Truly I should be ungrateful if I failed to mourn for the man who gave me my lovely heart. I should like to cry a little because Oz is gone, if you will kindly wipe away my tears, so that I shall not rust.'

'With pleasure,' she answered, and brought a towel at once. Then the Tin Woodman wept for several minutes, and she watched the tears carefully and wiped them away with the towel. When he had finished, he thanked her kindly and oiled himself thoroughly with his jeweled oil-can, to guard against mishap.

−Oz

I accepted the tissue from Dorothy. "Thanks.... Well, I was almost ready to receive the help that therapy would offer, but I needed a friend during these dark days. How you helped the Tin Man is a good picture of what people need from us when they're sad."

21
THE FIVE-YEAR ROAD
TO THE EMERALD CITY

So they found a cozy place under the trees where they slept well until the morning; and Dorothy dreamed of the Emerald City and of the good Wizard Oz, who would soon send her back to her own home again.

—Oz

Dorothy, it's almost time for us to reach the Emerald City! Just a few more adventures. We're getting close."

Dorothy smiled in response as we walked ahead of the three adult selves. The two of us would finish the story because as the move out of The 4Generation House began, the three adult selves were hopelessly at odds with each other and shifting erratically.

LEAVING THE 4GENERATION HOUSE

Despite the increasing number of dark days, I still had to work, figure out the logistics of moving, and worst of all, pack again. Telling the owners of The 4Generation House we would be moving sent me into panic mode for several days. How would we ever find a safe, affordable, handicap-accessible place near work?

We created a list of seventeen "needs and wants." It seemed impossible, but the day we walked through the condo for the first time, we realized all but one item had a check by it and that item wasn't a deal breaker. It felt like a modern-day miracle. It even had a walk-in closet. Our drive to work would only be minutes long, and in a few months my drive to and from therapy would also be short.

SAYING GOODBYE

We moved out of The 4Generation House the same week Paula moved across country. The memory of this week feels surreal. My ability to stay present was doubtful. Being present and surviving that level of emotion without complete collapse was probably impossible. The day she moved I went to my office, turned out the lights, and curled up in a fetal position on my couch. My daughter understood and brought me chocolate cake.

Reality sank in while curled up on the couch. My lifelong efforts had neither healed nor brought me one step closer to "normal." I couldn't understand why my friend's move completely devastated me, but the depth of my despair clearly wasn't healthy. Now I understand that those were the emotions of a small, abandoned child.

The dark cloud swallowed me whole. There hadn't ever been a single joyfully-greeted day, and pretending to have a joyful life was exhausting. The desperate thought of living out the remainder of my life in this agonizing state consumed me. Hope died there, but I willed myself off the couch with pure determination. When asked how I was doing, my answer was always, "Fine." My smile convinced everyone.

Repressed traumatic memories had begun surfacing, even without professional therapeutic care. Not seeking help when I did could have resulted in the pain releasing without any help to process it. Now understanding the amount of trauma my entire body and mind were holding, the danger is clear.

THE UNSEEN HOPE OF THERAPY

If it were possible, I would go back to the couch and tell my deeply troubled self how peaceful healing would one day feel. Sadly, this isn't possible, but it is possible to tell the hurting world: "If you were able to survive the evil inflicted on you and the internal turmoil caused by it, then you can survive healing." Even understanding the struggle, I would choose therapy again and repeat every grueling session to feel the powerful changes healing brought. But at the time, when I was curled up on the couch in my office, this wasn't even imaginable.

As the dark cloud consumed me, it never occurred to me that therapy would help. How is this possible? Whatever I believed therapy might accomplish for other people, I thought it certainly didn't have anything to do with my own consuming dark cloud. This complete disconnect (denial) astounds me!

In the two years since *BRAVE* was published, the notes from readers indicate that many others were not aware that trauma-induced mental health issues can heal—or what trauma-informed therapy looks like. *BRAVE* is now giving others the hope my tortured selves needed while in a fetal position on my office couch. The book is also helping others feel less lonely during the healing process. Their notes are like a comforting quilt of hope that I can now tuck around me.

> *Thank you for bravely and honestly sharing your story. I feel as though I am sitting with a friend when I read it, someone who knows what the struggle to resurrect from trauma feels like. Thank you for what you mean to me and countless others who have experienced trauma and are trying to find space just to breathe and be.*
> —a *BRAVE* reader (shared with permission)

WHERE *BRAVE* BEGAN

Without help, my only choice seemed to be crawling out of the dark pit one more time. The days leading up to our move kept marching forward. I managed to finish packing up our earthly possessions and move them into the condo.

Cleaning The 4Generation House proved to be an enormous effort. Our determination to leave the family's dream house in at least as good shape as when we moved in, proved exhausting. We cleaned, touched up paint, sanded and stained woodwork, shampooed carpets, and made repairs. We worked for days. After locking the door for the last time, my Facebook post said: "Last one standing, hand over the keys and drag the fallen family members out the door!"

It would be five more years before we left for Washington State. But *BRAVE* began while living in the condo. I walked into therapy at the end of October after visiting Paula. On the flight home, I sensed something was coming.

Here we could end this *BRAVE* prequel. But we still hadn't made it to the Emerald City. So much still lay ahead of us. We lived in the condo during my first year in therapy. I retired, but Scott continued working at the college. About the same time, my dad suggested he move to a nursing home. He realized the increasing difficulty in providing the necessary level of care. Thankfully, we were able to find him a place in a nursing home that met my very high expectations.

~

Dorothy's eyes were sympathetic as she said, "I can't imagine how difficult it must have been to move him into the nursing home."

I sighed. "Oh yes. But the facilities felt like the Hilton of nursing homes. Everyone loved him; he was well cared for; and he enjoyed having his favorite chair."

"How old was he when he moved there?" Dorothy asked.

"He celebrated his 100th birthday soon after moving in, and the facilities were perfect for his birthday celebration. Friends and relatives came from across the state and country."

Dorothy smiled, and I continued.

"Melinda and the grandkids moved to Washington State the next week. We moved out of the condo at the same time, and I spent two months in Washington helping them settle.

Upon my return, we bought the RV and moved into the RV park where Scott eventually became manager. So many changes in such a brief time! And my dad died eight months later. Life just kept throwing things at me."

I sighed loudly and continued. *"BRAVE, Jeannie's BRAVE Childhood*, and most of this book were written in the RV. My time was divided between Washington and Colorado and in many ways this prepared me for the eventual move. Then I wrote several endings for this book, but none of them felt right until the day Colorado ended. It is kind of strange how it happened."

Dorothy appreciated strange. She motioned toward my laptop computer, then she settled in to listen to the end of Colorado.

COLORADO ENDS

One seemingly normal, sunny March day, I was chatting with a friend on Messenger about how to end this book when Scott walked in holding a box.

"What's in the box?" I asked.

"My office things. They fired me."

And thus Colorado ended.

Once again, we stayed too long. What an unimaginable ending of both job and community! Our RV life had a Facebook page and a Website. My place of healing, in one shattering moment, was ripped out from under me by an inexplicable corporate decision, tainting our magnificent RV adventure with sadness.

Scott's deep concern for his employees, who also were losing their jobs and community, made the situation even more wrenching. Scott and I, the employees, and long-term residents of the RV park had suffered through two years of construction for the largest combined project ever undertaken by the city and county, and it still wasn't finished.

During that time we had lived with floods, mud, torn up streets, the constant beep of backing trucks, pounding jackhammers, and the presence of hundreds of construction workers. The area looked like the aftermath of Dorothy's cyclone after the construction project toppled over one hundred trees. It felt like my healing paradise died. Scott had kept the place afloat (literally) and a couple months earlier the president of the company had commended him for his work at a corporate meeting.

Then they fired him.

It made no sense, but Colorado was definitely over.

PLUNGED INTO CHAOS

Everything ended so abruptly. We had a plan for moving but not enough time to implement it. Once again, we became trapped in a cycle of powerlessness. A simple conversation and agreed-upon exit plan would have helped everyone involved.

We needed to leave quickly. Yes, our home (RV) was mobile, but we never intended to move it to Washington State. We had to sell it immediately, as well as the truck that we never planned to move. And then … well, it is amazing how much stuff one can own with only an RV and an office.

In ten days' time we packed our car, rented a small storage unit for the carload we would retrieve the following summer, and sold or gave away most of what we owned. In the middle of the chaos, we eked out time to spend with friends. It felt much like an episode of Dorothy's spinning cyclone, but we did have many good memories to take with us.

During our time in the RV park (before the construction) we had enjoyed our friends and the stories of hundreds of travelers who crossed our path. There I had held my first copies of both *BRAVE* and *Jeannie's BRAVE Childhood*. It felt sad to leave friends behind in such an abrupt way, but ready or not, we were on our way down the Yellow Brick Road to the Emerald City.

REACHING WASHINGTON

I hoped all the triggers involved in moving wouldn't send me backwards. Could I face the daunting task of moving to Washington State as optimistically as Dorothy handled the journey to Oz?

The sun shone bright and the birds sang sweetly, and Dorothy did not feel nearly so bad as you might think a little girl would who had been suddenly whisked away from her own country and set down in the midst of a strange land.

–Oz

We spent four silent days driving to Washington. Weber proved to be a great traveler, but I was fighting a cold, and our wounded spirits left little room for enjoying the trip. We dodged winter storms all the way across country, but during the last leg of the trip through the Columbia Gorge, we watched as multiple rainbows stretched across the river. Maybe we could go over those rainbows to where our troubles would melt like lemon drops. It did feel like God smiled down on us as the rainbows appeared.

The move proved to be a daunting transition, but my healing did make a difference. I wasn't the same and no longer needed my dissociative structures to navigate life and distance myself from another painful episode. Life threw me a huge curve but did not steal the healing I had worked so hard to gain.

Everything I needed was right inside me. Like the Scarecrow, I always had a brain (Non Janyne); like the Tin Man, a heart (Jane); and like the Lion, courage (Janyne). These were always in "me." They had helped me the best they could. Now healed and able to share life together, they could help me live life versus distancing myself from it.

Just as Dorothy discovered each companion and helped

them find who they were created to be (with help from the Wizard), I likewise helped my three adult selves heal and become a healthy, whole "me." Together we are stronger than the three adult selves could have imagined as they lived out my life in a tenuous and increasingly antagonistic coexistence.

Sadness tinged my goodbye to Colorado much like Dorothy's departure from Oz. She would return to Kansas a very different child because of her excursion to Oz. She would miss her friends; but there really was no place like home. I hadn't ever lived in Seattle, yet it felt like coming home to my own Emerald City. Now we would need to build a new life.

～

Dorothy watched me finish typing and said, "Leaving Colorado was sad, wasn't it?"

"It was hard to leave all my friends and support. But having our family there in Seattle, waiting for us to arrive, felt like going home, albeit arriving in another cyclone. Tapping my heels together three times would have been much easier. But I was OK and knew how to care for myself now without needing to avoid the overwhelming emotions. Feeling angry and sad didn't drown me like it had during most of my life."

Dorothy leaned forward. "You know, Glinda told me if I had known the power in the silver shoes, I could have gone back to Aunt Em the very first day in Oz. If you had gotten help and understood everything you needed was inside you—just like the Lion, Scarecrow, and Tin Man, you could have healed when you were much younger."

"Dorothy, you are right! I did have everything necessary to thrive but needed help to understand the frightening feelings inside my body after the abuse. This is what mothers or caregivers should do for children, but my mother wasn't able. I am grateful Dr. Sue helped me. She seemed to be a combination of the Wizard and Glinda."

221

Dorothy laughed. "Now that's a strange combination!"

I laughed with her. "Right? She may not appreciate the description when she reads this, but she will laugh! It means she was both kind and wise. My life held much pain, but her care and wisdom helped me turn those experiences into a beautiful *BRAVE* story—actually several *BRAVE* stories now."

Suddenly, surrounded by a couple dozen of my child, teen, young adult, and adult selves, we all understood this book had finally come to a perfect conclusion. Everyone began hugging Dorothy and thanking her for helping us reach the Emerald City. Then as I watched,

> *Glinda the Good stepped down from her ruby throne to give the little girl a good-bye kiss, and Dorothy thanked her for all the kindness she had shown to her friends and herself. Dorothy now took Toto up solemnly in her arms, and having said one last good-bye she clapped the heels of her shoes together three times, saying: 'Take me home…!'*
>
> –Oz

We all stared at the spot where Dorothy vanished and were surprised to see that Alice now stood there instead—with a decidedly impatient expression on her face. "Time for the next book!" she announced. "We are not done saying important things."

She marched off through the looking glass to the next book as we all glanced at each other in surprise, then ran to catch up. Alice was on a mission to help others understand children (and adults) whose outer lives and inner lives feel so different on the two sides of fractured dissociative mirrors. She appeared eager to begin!

EPILOGUE
THE EMERALD CITY PORCH

The next morning, as soon as the sun was up, they started on their way, and soon saw a beautiful green glow in the sky just before them. 'That must be the Emerald City,' said Dorothy. As they walked on, the green glow became brighter and brighter, and it seemed that at last they were nearing the end of their travels.

–Oz

The journey down the Yellow Brick Road had finally brought Scott and me to the Emerald City where life, though not perfect, would be filled with the abundant life for which I had longed. The abundant life, symbolized by the Emerald City, was possible because of healing. The repressed traumatic pain, that had kept me fractured since childhood, no longer held me in its grip. There would always be times when my emotions would overwhelm me, but my toolbox was now filled with healthy ways to process. One of those ways would continue to be conversations with my inner selves, conversations which often turned to storytelling and reframing. It seems fitting, since this book began with a form of storytelling "on the porch," to conclude that way also. The characters are the same, but the setting is now the Emerald City.

We had been in the Seattle area for eight months before the seven-year-old Girl with the Hammer found the perfect spot to reconstruct the porch. She christened it "The Emerald City Porch." It felt perfect and would now become the imagined place for all future gatherings of my inner selves. Finding it was magical.

Scott and I were invited to spend a day touring several hotels in downtown Seattle. While taking a mid-tour break in a room on the 45th floor of the Hyatt Regency, I stood looking out a window, awestruck by the panoramic view of the city spread out below and Mt. Rainier rising majestically in the distance.

While gazing, I sensed that the small builder (my seven-year-old child self) found this to be a perfect place for a porch. I felt her standing poised with her hammer, exuding excitement. Then the imagined porch began to take shape. My inner selves had met in kitchens, around campfires, and on a porch in Virginia, but now this would become our home place for meetings. The amenities were exquisite, the view spectacular.

It is amazing how quickly a child can build a porch in her imagination! Before long, we were ready for everyone to gather. We invited Dorothy back from Kansas for the opening ceremony. The Lion, the Tin Man, and the Scarecrow, who were always welcome, journeyed from Oz to join in the festivities.

The three adult selves surveyed the porch with eager anticipation. Janyne enjoyed seeing all the places to explore in the city below, Non Janyne became enthralled with the delightfully tidy amenities, and Jane absorbed the breathtaking view.

Dorothy stood at the window for some time before exclaiming, "Look! I can see the Yellow Brick Road!"

There the road was, clear as a sunny Seattle day. The Yellow Brick Road wound past Mt. Rainier, through the Puyallup Valley, along Puget Sound and appeared to end at the foot of the Space Needle—right in the heart of the Emerald City of Seattle.

"Traveling in Oz would have been easier if I could have had a bird's-eye view like this," Dorothy said.

'True, Dorothy. We can't always see where the road is taking us."

When Ten arrived, Jane led her to the window to see the view.

"It feels like I can see forever," Ten whispered quietly.

Jane smiled. "Kind of like our life. We couldn't see much because the trauma blocked our view. But now after healing, we can look back and see so much more clearly—just like this view high above the city."

"I wonder if it is like this for God," Ten said. "Do you think God could see healing, out in the distant future, like we can see Mt. Rainier from here?"

Jane started to answer, but Jesus stepped in instead (he is ever present, you know). "Yes, Ten. From the time you were little, I could see a day when your world would understand trauma well enough to help you, and I knew you would never give up until you got there. You have been quite determined ever since you were little."

Ten grinned. Jesus was always there, even when she didn't know it. Then she turned serious. "Jesus, when we talk like this, it feels like I can know you now like I've seen others know you. What some people did to me kept us from talking. But now I understand; you were always there. Being a kid is so confusing sometimes. I thought *God* loved me, but *you* didn't. Maybe it was Nine's problem with the song."

Nine, who arrived in time to hear the conversation, agreed. "Yes, 'Jesus Loves Me.' That song made me angry because I thought it wasn't true."

Suddenly, from across the room, a younger voice started singing

> *Jesus loves me this I know*
> *He came to me and told me so.*
> *Big and small to him belong.*
> *They are small*
> *His love is strong.*
> *Yes, Jesus loved me,*
> *Yes, Jesus loves me,*

Yes, loved me always
He came and told me so.

Jesus walked over and knelt down to the level of the singing child and laughed with delight. "Ah, Seven, you were always recreating songs while you stored the boxes in the Cave of Memories. The songs helped you, didn't they?"

The child giggled. "Sometimes I didn't know the right words and just filled in ones that made sense; but yes, sometimes I rewrote them because I didn't like what they said."

Jesus looked fondly at the small, opinionated child. "Well, just keep rewriting them!" Then, to the Storyteller he said, "And you keep writing books!" The two children grinned at each other. They often collaborated, but were surprised Jesus knew this.

Turning to Non Janyne, Jesus said, "This is a much better book because you and Jane and Janyne all worked together with the Storyteller."

Non Janyne agreed. "It needed to be all three adult voices, but it still lacked something until we had Ten's story. Before that I had been over analyzing in the writing of this book, because nothing made sense without Ten's story."

Considering this, Jane asked, "In what way did Ten's story change this book?" (Sometimes she sounded very therapist-esque.)

Everyone watched Non Janyne, sensing she was the one to answer the question. Ten and Non Janyne exchanged a knowing look before Non Janyne answered. "Ten is the part of me that gave up on Jesus. Odd to spend my life in Bible colleges not really believing Jesus made any difference."

Realizing she was talking about Jesus as if he wasn't there, Non Janyne apologized. Then, looking directly at him, she continued. For me, living a life of faith meant accepting that there wasn't any possibility of feeling any differently. If faith alone could change the turmoil inside me, then it would have been changed; so I concluded that the inner turmoil was just *me* and not changeable.

Since I was little, it was important to just get up every day and do what was expected of me—to live my life. How I *felt* didn't matter. The message the church gave me was that the turmoil was *sin*—just like the camp counselor told Ten. Until Ten told her story, I didn't understand how angry the word "sin" made me. In the first manuscript I wrote for this book, I kept analyzing as I tried to figure that out, but it wasn't ever going to make sense without Ten's story. Deep inside me, *I* knew it wasn't sin; but who was going to believe me?"

Ten nodded. "When the camp counselor said I was lying and that the abuse I told her about really didn't happen ... well, after that I thought no one else in the church would ever believe me, either. She said my truth-telling was sin, and she insisted I ask for forgiveness. All the other children were asking Jesus to forgive them for things like talking back or fighting with brothers or sisters ... not for telling the truth."

"That's right, Ten," Non Janyne continued. "How could we believe the church would ever help us after that? To live in the church, we needed to forever keep our secrets, accept our sinfulness, and be what others wanted us to be. We certainly could never be who we *are*. No one would ever understand there were so many of us."

Teen Jane sighed. "I thought the voices in my head were demons."

In a sad voice Jesus asked, "What do you believe now?"

With a look of gratitude, Teen Jane answered, "Well, it certainly wasn't demons. It was small hurting children. It also wasn't my *fault*. How sad that the lack of understanding about trauma and teachings about sin and spiritual warfare only made my life more miserable. It just kept getting worse ... until now. Thank you for leading us to Dr. Sue so we could understand."

Non Janyne and Ten stood up and called everyone to stand by the window. There were child selves, teen selves, young adult selves, and adults. They all gazed out the window as Non Janyne glanced at Jesus and began talking.

"Teen Janyne is right. The lack of understanding about the effects of trauma only made it worse. We can help the church do better. We were created as one, but trauma divided us into many. We will always be many and now that we have healed, it is exactly who we want to be. We can live as one person—because it works better that way. But here in the Emerald City Porch, we are free to be many. And together, we can help our hurting world. We are one Janyne—but made of many."

Jesus smiled at the group. "I will never ask you to be anything but who you are. You have gained understanding of the coping mechanisms that enable humans to dissociate and split when the pain becomes too great. There should be no shame in this. Others need to know it is possible to heal and live the abundant life—even in parts. There are others who do not understand and are hiding in fear. They need hope."

Ten gazed deep into Jesus' eyes. "You love us *all*, don't you?"

Jesus smiled. "Yes, I do. All of you. Every part of you. My original intent was not for you to be in so many parts, but trauma caused you to split. Jeannie's imagination created quite the survival team. You are delightfully more."

Janyne giggled. "It's like Alice, but we got more muchier instead of less muchier. We certainly haven't lost our muchness."

'You're not the same as you were before,' he said. 'You were much more ... muchier ... you've lost your muchness.'

–Tim Burton's 2010 *Alice in Wonderland* movie

The entire Emerald City Porch laughed and in one very excited voice yelled, "We are muchier!"

~

Yes, I am certainly "muchier." Like King David looking back over his life and seeing all the varied ways he was prepared for his role as king, I can see how God has used my experiences to prepare me for this present time (the good experiences God desired for me and the tragic ones God never desired, planned, or even "allowed"). My background and story can provide unique perspectives. God wastes nothing while working to help our hurting world.

Affirmation of that truth arrived in an e-mail while I was finishing this writing. The first sentence jumped off the screen: "Your story is not wasted."

The sentence took me back to a day during the first year of therapy when memories were just beginning to surface and my struggles with the church became evident. This struggle, now better understood, came out in multiple ways as described in this book. At the time these struggles didn't seem trauma related, but instead appeared to be adult problems mostly related to the diminishment of women's gifts in church-related ministries. Out of the blue, I said, "My story will not be wasted."

In that moment it truly felt prophetic as I added, "I will write a book about this one day." Until the e-mail arrived, this memory remained buried amid hundreds of hours of therapy. God sent me a reminder in five simple words: "Your story is not wasted."

The process of authoring this book proved to be greater than the other two books put together. It took time to understand how my church-related struggles revolved around a ten-year-old child's camp memory. With this understanding, it became a story about a devastated child determined to serve a God she wasn't sure could love her. This makes little sense aside from those church members and camp counselors who truly cared about her—even when they got things wrong. How much better it could have been if they had understood the effects of trauma and how to help her! It wasn't a lack of care; it was a lack of understanding.

No, Ten, your story isn't wasted. Thank you for helping me understand my steadfast belief that the problem wasn't spiritual—despite all the messages to the contrary. This book needed your story. Thank you for being *BRAVE*.

ADDENDUM 1
A Synopsis of *BRAVE*

In the fall of 2014, I began three years of intensive therapy. The book, *BRAVE: A Personal Story of Healing Childhood Trauma*, is the story of how I, with the help of a skilled and caring therapist, Dr. Susan Kwiecien, unraveled my childhood story of inadequate attachment and extensive sexual abuse that began in a home day care at the age of three. As my subconscious began splitting to hold the pain and trauma, my dissociative coping mechanisms made me a target for perpetrators until I reached my young adult years.

The use of EMDR (Eye Movement and Desensitization Reprocessing) allowed me to find the truth under the cover stories in which I had subconsciously created non traumatic endings to hide traumatic memories from consciousness.

During the first EMDR session, when working through a childhood memory, Dr. Sue asked me to return to my adult self and I asked, "Which one?" My three adult parts, Janyne, Non Janyne, and Jane (known as the Three Chairs) made a perfect three-point landing in that instant and therapy became intensive as we worked together to heal memories and integrate.

My final year as a college professor was completed while my inner world held so tightly for so many years began to completely unravel. I lived in terror that anyone would find out I was in therapy. I retired at the end of the year and spent the next two years focused on healing trauma and integrating over twenty parts which had split in order to survive the trauma.

Dissociative Disorders are among the most challenging mental illnesses to heal. The process of healing described in *BRAVE* required my determination and a high level of therapeutic intervention and care. I am grateful to both myself and Dr. Sue. I worked very, very hard, but could not have survived without her skill and care.

During the second year of therapy, the children began to surface and tell their stories. Trauma had frozen children at every developmental stage. Each child played a specific role in my dissociative system and held a core traumatic memory. As we healed the core memories, they became healed versions of themselves and began to write their stories which were published in *Jeannie's BRAVE Childhood.*

Another year of therapy was required to reach the point where I could begin to be the mother to the inner children—the mother they had always needed, but my own mother was incapable of being. This was the final phase of integration.

To say that it was a harrowing journey cannot even begin to describe the darkness through which I walked. It is common for the healing of dissociative disorders to take over ten years in therapy-if ever healed. It is really a journey of treating multiple clients. Sometimes neither Dr. Sue or I were sure who had come to therapy.

The Cliff was the pivotal memory which separated my childhood from my adult life. This memory surfaced late in the second year of therapy and is the starting point for this book. It was the day that changed everything.

My ability to live at two levels enabled me to remain somewhat functional, except for the weeks and months when I hardly left the bed. Yet, in the midst of this, I traveled extensively and began to tell family and friends the secrets I had so carefully held for sixty years. In the words of Dr. Sue, "Janyne McConnaughey may be the most resilient of the resilient clients I saw during many years of therapy."

Scott, calmly stood beside me as I fell down the rabbit hole in my head and together we healed and survived my retirement, buying and moving into an RV, the death of my father, my daughter and grandchildren moving, and the loss of his job. We healed together and grew stronger as he became General Manager of the RV Resort where we lived and I published *BRAVE*. We truly rose from the ashes of our life—but the story continues in this prequel to *BRAVE.*

ADDENDUM 2
The Foreword to *BRAVE*

Janyne McConnaughey may be the most resilient of the resilient clients I saw during many years of therapy. She is also a storyteller. From infancy to young adult years, she had held inside all the intensity of feelings, shame, helplessness, and meaning that were part of each experience of trauma she endured. To cope, she repressed memories detached from feelings, unknowingly created personas to hold the feelings and trauma experiences, and rose above the pain to live the life she was expected to live. This explains the two selves she describes at each age. One held the trauma experience and the other "rose above."

The story she tells is the cognitive retelling of intense therapy—a tortuous journey that uncovered layers of trauma experience held with all the intensity of feelings and the meaning of the experience. The therapy used was EMDR (Eye Movement Desensitization and Reprocessing), a therapy treatment recognized worldwide, that targets unprocessed memories, body sensations, and the meaning of the trauma experience, which are held in the primitive, limbic brain where the fight-or-flight instinct and the feeling centers are located. When trauma has occurred, the instinctual readiness to protect overrides cognition, so anything resembling an emotionally-repressed experience can trigger an intense reaction that can feel overwhelming, confusing and shameful.

Experiencing herself as brave at each of the ages as she processed was a critical piece of her therapy. Janyne was an exceptionally brave child, young adult, and therapy client.

Between therapy sessions, she wrote volumes as she processed what emerged from each intense therapy session and prepared for the next session. She bravely stayed with therapy when she wanted it to be done, and stayed until she was able to connect understanding and compassion with all of herself.

Interestingly, Janyne's Ph.D. is in education with Early Childhood as her focus. Now, with this background, she is ready to use her own experience to help others. This involves understanding the child's experience of connection to self and others. When initial attachment to significant others in a young child's life is missing, and trauma occurs, this connection is absent. Janyne's story shows a path to integration and wholeness.

–Susan M. Kwiecien, Ph.D., LMFT, EMDR II, Retired

Author's note:

My deepest gratitude goes to Dr. Sue and all therapists who devote their lives to helping others heal from childhood trauma. Your dedication helps the world heal one client at a time, but the effects reach around the world and into future generations! The attentive care I received follows me wherever my path takes me—including the Emerald City.

ADDENDUM 3
ACEs Research

The Adverse Childhood Experiences (ACE) Study[36] was instrumental in understanding many of my lifelong effects of early childhood trauma. Excellent resources are available online about this groundbreaking research study conducted by Kaiser and the CDC in the 1990s. The following partial list explains the ways my ACE Score of five out of ten affected my life. The relative stability of my life mitigated many potentially negative health and well being outcomes detailed by the ACE Study. The higher the ACE Score, the higher the risk of these outcomes (and many more):

- Depression: Pervasive throughout my lifetime.
- Health-related quality of life: A high correlation exists between trauma and obesity, which was a constant issue for me as an adult.
- Financial stress: Embedded survival strategies and negative internalized messages often show up in financial decisions.
- Multiple sexual partners: Vulnerability caused me to be a target, and then I blamed myself.
- Suicide attempts: I attempted suicide at the age of 23.
- Unintended pregnancies: A miscarriage may have occurred.
- Pregnancy was a real possibility.
- Risk for sexual violence: Multiple incidents.
- Poor academic achievement: I was an over achieving under achiever![37]

---

36. See "Adverse Childhood Experiences" (ACEs): https://www.cdc.gov/violenceprevention/acestudy/

37. McConnaughey, J., "The Overachieving Underachiever," *Therapeutic Parenting Journal* (ATN, April 2018).

ADDENDUM 4
Suicide Prevention Resources

Many behaviors make sense if you can understand them as coping mechanisms designed for self-preservation ... even suicide. The first time I heard this, I was incredulous. How could I have almost died by trying to take care of myself? As I thought about it though, it made sense. The purpose of my suicide attempt at the cliff was to end the pain which had become excruciatingly unbearable. I didn't want to die; I wanted to stop the pain.

Over my lifetime, suicidal ideation was subconsciously utilized as a coping mechanism. Without being cognizant of this, I believed that if the pain got too bad, there was a way out. This thought was oddly comforting; I had the power to stop the pain. Believing no one else could help me, it was still possible to help myself. It wasn't logical and could have had tragic ramifications for me and all who knew and loved me. The stigma and judgment surrounding suicide prevented me from seeking the help I desperately needed and blinded me to the fact that there were resources and ways to find help.

The following resources are intended to help those who are in a place to be hope providers to others. If I had been able to speak to someone, would they have had the information and resources to help me? That question prompted me to include this addendum. There are many other resources, but this list provided by Kiersten Adkins, M.A., LPC, (Executive Director, Pathway to Hope), provides a starting place.

National Suicide Prevention Lifeline
800-273-TALK (8255)
https://suicidepreventionlifeline.org/
The Lifeline provides 24/7, free and confidential support for people in distress, prevention and crisis resources for you or your loved ones, and best practices for professionals.

The Lifesaving Church: Faith Communities and Suicide Prevention by Rachael A. Keefe
https://chalicepress.com/products/the-lifesaving-church
Book Preview: "Is your church prepared to save lives? Every year, millions of people engage in suicidal activity, yet the Church remains largely silent around mental health and suicide prevention. Pastor Rachael Keefe shares her own painful story of life-long depression and suicidality to help churches recognize and respond to those suffering."

My3 App
https://my3app.org/
"Who are your 3? Is it your sister? Your therapist? Maybe even a neighbor down the street? Download MY3 to make sure that your 3 are there to help you when you need them most. With MY3, you define your network and your plan to stay safe. With MY3 you can be prepared to help yourself and reach out to others when you are having thoughts of suicide."

Article from Help Guide
"Are You Feeling Suicidal?" Jaelline Jaffe, Ph.D., Lawrence Robinson, and Jeanne Segal, Ph.D.
https://www.helpguide.org/articles/suicide-prevention/are-you-feeling-suicidal.htm (Last updated: October 2019)
A comprehensive article that addresses the reasons behind suicidal thoughts, actions to take, ways to cope, things to avoid, paths to recovery, and resources. "Even though your pain may seem overwhelming and permanent at the moment, there are ways to deal with suicidal thoughts and feelings and overcome the pain."

ADDENDUM 5
Trauma-Informed Church Ministries

Understanding the effects of childhood abuse is essential in ministering to both churches and communities. Study Guides which cover the following questions as related to specific chapters are available upon request at drjanynemc@gmail.com The author also considers speaking venues for addressing these questions.

• How do we reconcile the research on the physical and behavioral effects of Adverse Childhood Experience (ACE) with a Christian view of sin?

• How can we encourage spiritual growth without creating additional shame and feelings of worthlessness?

• How can survival coping mechanisms be distinguished from conscious choices?

• How can understanding the neurobiology of trauma and trauma-informed care aid in leading others to the abundant life Jesus intended for every person?

• How can the spiritual strength of survivors enrich churches and communities?

ACKNOWLEDGEMENTS

When I know I'm going to work on a cover, I practically run to the computer! After working with words for so long, it's lovely to do something that's creative yet also the professional equivalent of scribbling in your own coloring book.

–Teresa Medeiors

The *BRAVE* book covers are an invitation to my writing. They are a combination of my "scribbled" vision and my sister-in-law, Kay McConnuaughey's artistry (with credit to the photographers). My vision was that *BRAVE* book covers would symbolically represent some part of my story. I am grateful for the remarkable way Kay brought my symbols to life (the bicycle, the chair, and now the typewriter). I am also grateful for my publisher (Cladach Publishing: Catherine and Larry Lawton) who trusted my intuition and then embraced the designs. All of us together have created three book covers that bring joy to me and my readers.

I am also grateful for my long-time friends who were my support base as I tried to live the complicated life shared in this book. I have mentioned two (Mary Herman and Paula Scarbrough) and alluded to several others, but the entire list would be far too long to include, and I would surely forget someone important (but they may see themselves!)

Though not named in the book, I specifically acknowledge Norma Gillming, who left this world as I completed the final revision of this book. She was my mentor, pastor's wife, colleague, counselor, and friend. Her support and guidance proved crucial while raising my children. Our laughter, adventures, time spent at the lake cabin, ministry-related projects, and Boggle® games are some of my fondest memories. The more I wrote, the clearer it became that God's provision of hope for survivors can only come through relationships.

The year before moving to the Seattle area, was an important year of stabilizing. I processed my childhood trauma at breakneck speed and needed time to rest, write, and adjust. I travelled less (except to see my family in the Seattle area), and spent time testing my wings. My time with local friends, Kay Schaff, Leslie Mikesell, Heather Thompson, Laura Harper, and Emma Harris provided diversion and opportunity to grow. I am grateful for the good times we shared as I became comfortable with my healed (and healing) self. Any who embark on a healing journey as intense as mine that I describe in *BRAVE*, desperately need friends who are comfortable with our stories. Without these friends, I might have turned into a total recluse!

Also, that year, Carnelian Coffee in Old Colorado City became my favorite meeting spot, and the owner, Kate Firoved, honored me by serving my coffee in a bicycle mug. It was also there that I joined my first book club sponsored by the nearby Carnegie Library. I will miss the great discussions led by Joe Paisley. The theme for my last Book Club was "March Memoirs" and *BRAVE* was one of the optional books. Thanks to those who read! (And thanks to the other Book Clubs who have also read *BRAVE*!)

Two friends helped me work through the physical struggles caused by trauma. Thank you, Hilary Sturtevant for being patient with my tense hands during ten years of manicures, and Rocke Hjersman for your skilled, trauma-sensitive massages that helped me continue to release trauma from my body.

It was at the Buffalo Lodge Bicycle Resort that I spotted the bicycle which inspired the cover for *BRAVE*. When Colorado ended abruptly the resort's owner, Torrie Jennings, offered us lodging as we prepared to move. As hard as those ten days were, it could have been so much worse! This gesture of kindness will never be forgotten!

And most importantly, thank you to my family who have found themselves taken captive in the stories in this book (husband, Scott; children, Melinda and Eric; daughter-in-law, Kelly; grandchildren, Sabien and Aria; Grandpa Jenkins, who now watches from Heaven; and all our many pets—and the duck). I have done my best to ask permission for the stories. Without these loved ones and pets, my life and stories lose their richness. You are the ones who helped me know life was worth living on those dark days which had no explanation. Your support for me as I try to encourage others to heal is everything!

My gratitude goes to three organizations that have given me a glimpse of how human efforts can change the world: Bridge Hope (Co-founders, John and Jessa Crisp); Attachment & Trauma Network (Too many individuals to name, but thank you Julie Beem, Executive Director and Dr. Melissa Sadin, Creating Trauma Sensitive Schools); and Pathway to Hope (Executive Director, Kiersten Adkins).

Finding a church which feels safe is not easy for survivors. Thank you to Bethel Church of the Nazarene (Spanaway, WA: Pastor, Chris Whighaman) for welcoming my family and reminding me of the many ways multigenerational church members cared for me as a child and teen.

The richness of my life is evident in the list of those who took time to read and edit or provide feedback on this book. I thank Susan Hyder (friends since fifth grade and college roommates), Richard Ferguson (friends since eighth grade), Susan Armstrong (friends since middle school), Al Magnusum (cousin and friend), Chris Phillips (friend and colleague, Colorado), Kiersten Adkins (former student and friend, Colorado), and Miriam Chickering (a recent gift of friendship as a result of *BRAVE* networking).

Finally, to all my supportive friends (including Kathy Jordon, whose porch inspired the prologue); *BRAVE* readers, reviewers, and endorsers; therapists, educators and other professionals who have been recommending *BRAVE*, I say thank you! Your belief in me keeps me writing. You help me be *BRAVE*!

ABOUT THE AUTHOR

Janyne McConnaughey, Ph.D. retired from a forty-year career in education while healing from the attachment wounding and trauma she experienced as a child. During therapy, she wrote her way to healing and now is redeeming her story by helping others to understand the lifelong effects of childhood trauma and insecure attachment.

Along with *BRAVE: A Personal Story of Healing Childhood Trauma*, the companion book, *Jeannie's Brave Childhood: Behavior and Healing through the Lens of Attachment and Trauma*, and *A BRAVE Life: A Personal Story of Survival, Resilience, Faith, and Hope after Childhood Trauma*, Janyne is also working on several future books dealing with specific trauma and attachment related topics.

Janyne serves on the Board of Directors for the Attachment & Trauma Network and is a frequent guest blogger for the organization. She also blogs at her own Website (Janyne.org), and for other organizations addressing trauma and attachment. Though Janyne devotes most of her time to writing, she also speaks to educators and to church ministry leaders, at conferences, schools, and through podcast interviews. She can be contacted through her Website.

Janyne enjoys living in and exploring the Seattle area with her husband, Scott, children, grandchildren, and her rescue dog, Weber. Her favorite activity is to follow her GPS to "green spaces" along the coast of Puget Sound.

To Find Janyne online, visit:

Website: http://Janyne.org
Twitter: @janynetweets
Instagram: https://www.instagram.com/drjanynemc/
Facebook: http://www.facebook.com/janynemc/

Lightning Source UK Ltd.
Milton Keynes UK
UKHW010636051021
391704UK00003B/451